# Worship as My Weapon

*Living Victoriously through the Power of Praise*

*Gerard Assey*

**Worship as My Weapon:**
***Living Victoriously through the Power of Praise***

By

Gerard Assey



*Published by:*
Gerard Assey
19/18, Palli Arasan Street
Anna Nagar East
Chennai - 600 102

**ISBN:** 978-81-986974-4-8

# Table of Contents

## Disclaimer:

*Any resemblance (names, characters, and scenarios used in this book, including testimonies and personal stories) to actual persons, living or dead, or actual events is purely coincidental. These examples are used solely for illustrative and teaching purposes.*

*The intent is to inspire and equip readers, not to depict real individuals or specific events. No harm or misrepresentation is intended.*

# Preface

Worship is not just a song we sing. It's not confined to melodies, lyrics, or stages filled with lights and music. Worship is warfare. It is a weapon forged in the fire of surrender, wielded in the secret place, and sharpened in the wilderness of trials. It is the language of heaven and the heartbeat of those who have chosen to align themselves with the purposes of God on the earth.

This book was birthed out of a deep stirring in my spirit—a longing to see the Body of Christ rise up in power, not through worldly strength, but through the power of praise. We live in a world teeming with battles: personal, emotional, spiritual, cultural, and global. Too often, we try to fight these battles with fleshly tools—logic, complaint, manipulation, or silence. But heaven has always operated differently. Throughout Scripture, we find an unshakable truth: when God's people worship, things shift. Chains break. Walls crumble. Enemies scatter. Heaven invades earth.

**"WORSHIP AS MY WEAPON-** ***Living Victoriously Through the Power of Praise*****"** is an invitation—a call to arms. Not with swords of steel or armies of men, but with lifted hands and surrendered hearts. It is a journey into the revelation that praise is not passive—it is powerful. It is not ornamental—it is offensive against darkness. Worship is how we enthrone God in the midst of our chaos, how we fight battles we cannot see, and how we walk in the victory already won by Christ.

This book is for the weary worshiper and the seasoned psalmist. It's for the young child learning to lift their voice and the grandmother who has warred in worship for decades. It is for worship leaders and pastors, for parents and teachers, for soldiers and saints. Whether you worship with a guitar or with a whisper, whether from a pulpit or a prison cell, this message is for you.

Inside these pages, you'll find biblical teaching, real-life stories, prophetic insight, declarations of faith, and practical tools to equip you for a lifestyle of victorious worship. My desire is not simply to inform you, but to ignite you—to stir your spirit and open your eyes to the authority you carry when you praise.

As you journey through these chapters, I encourage you to read not just with your mind but with your spirit. Let the Word of God speak. Let the testimonies inspire. Let the worship declarations become your own. And above all, rise up. Pick up your weapon. Open your mouth. And worship.

Because when you do—heaven moves.

In Christ's victory,
**Gerard Assey**
*Servant. Worshiper. Warrior.*

# The Battle is Real – A Call to Worship

The air may feel calm, the world may look organized on the outside, but make no mistake—there is a battle raging in the unseen realm. Not a battle of swords or bullets, but one of dominion, allegiance, and worship. Behind every discouragement, fear, temptation, and chaos lies a deeper conflict: Who will you worship?

In a world of increasing darkness, confusion, and spiritual numbness, many believers are waking up to a powerful truth that has been too long forgotten—worship is not just a slow song before a sermon; worship is warfare. It is heaven's strategy for victory on earth. It is not a warm-up; it is the war front. And God is raising up worshippers, not just singers, who understand that when they lift their voices, they shake foundations and shift atmospheres.

**Why Worship Is More Than a Song**

It's easy to reduce worship to the music segment in a church service—four songs, a bridge, and a chorus. But true worship predates instruments and lyrics. It existed before humans were created, before earth was formed. Worship is the language of heaven, the native expression of the Kingdom. Angels cry, "Holy, Holy, Holy," not because it's poetic, but because it's truth, and truth compels worship.

In John 4:23-24, Jesus tells the Samaritan woman that the Father is seeking worshippers—not worship events, not perfect voices—but hearts that worship in spirit and in truth. That one statement shattered centuries of tradition and ritual and revealed the

heart of God. Worship isn't a genre; it's a posture. It's not about volume; it's about value—how much we value Him.
Worship is the surrender of our entire being to the One who is worthy. In Romans 12:1, Paul urges us to present our bodies as living sacrifices—this is our reasonable act of worship. Worship, then, is not confined to music; it's the offering of our lives in daily obedience and trust, especially in the midst of battle.

**Heaven's Strategy for Victory on Earth**
Heaven fights differently than we do. Where we wield logic and retaliation, heaven wields worship. In 2 Chronicles 20, King Jehoshaphat faced an impossible military threat from multiple nations. His strategy? He didn't position his strongest warriors on the front lines—he placed worshippers. Men dressed not in armor but in holiness, singing "Give thanks to the Lord, for His love endures forever." And as they sang, the Lord set ambushes against their enemies.
Victory was won not through brute strength but by exalting God in the face of fear. Worship confused the enemy, realigned the people to God's presence, and shifted the outcome of the battle. This principle is not confined to ancient stories—it remains true today. When we worship, we're not escaping reality; we are enforcing Kingdom reality. Worship declares, "God is greater than this problem, this pain, this prison." It invites the presence of God, and where He is, there is liberty (2 Corinthians 3:17).

**Real-Life Call: Ordinary People, Extraordinary Worship**
Mica, a young nurse in rural Kenya, found herself overwhelmed during the COVID pandemic. Day after

day, she watched lives slip through her hands. She stopped singing, stopped praying. But one day, while sitting outside her tiny clinic, she felt a nudge in her spirit: Sing. She resisted. But the voice persisted. Finally, with a cracked voice and trembling heart, she began to sing an old hymn in Swahili. As her voice lifted, so did the heaviness. Peace invaded her like a rushing wind. That day, four critical patients turned a corner unexpectedly. Doctors called it coincidence. Mira knew it was worship that had shifted the atmosphere.

Joshua, a retired army veteran from Bristol, battled PTSD in silence. Nightmares, depression, and rage haunted him. Medications failed. Therapy helped some, but he still felt empty. One evening, he wandered into a church and sat in the back. The worship team began to sing, not loud or perfect, but with sincerity. Tears rolled down his face. It was like someone unlocked a door inside him. He didn't understand what was happening, but he felt safe for the first time in years. That night began his journey—not to becoming a singer, but a worshipper. And slowly, the grip of darkness loosened.

These stories are not rare. Around the world, believers are discovering that when all else fails, worship still works. Worship is how we fight our battles—not with clenched fists, but with raised hands. Not by retreating, but by revering.

**The Vision and Purpose of This Book**

This book is a call to awaken the worshipping warrior in every believer. It's not written for musicians alone, but for all who desire to live in victory. Whether you're a mother raising children, a student facing pressures, a leader battling burnout, or a pastor walking through spiritual deserts—this book is for you.

Its pages will walk you through the theology, strategy, and application of worship as warfare. We'll explore biblical examples from both Old and New Testaments. We'll look at the life of Jesus and the apostles. We'll meet fictional characters facing modern-day battles, just like you.

Each chapter will be both instructional and inspirational. You will find truth, but also testimonies. You will be challenged, but also equipped. Exercises, worship prompts, Scripture references, and real-life applications will help you grow in your identity as a worshipper and fighter.

The purpose is simple: to equip an army of worshippers who know how to bring heaven to earth—through worship. This is not emotional hype. It is spiritual discipline, built on biblical truth. It's time to lift your voice. Time to raise your hands. Time to worship not just on mountaintops but in valleys, storms, prisons, and warzones.

*Because the battle is real.*

*But so is the victory.*

*And worship is our weapon.*

# PART I:
# LAYING THE FOUNDATION
## Understanding Worship

# Chapter 1:
# What Is Worship? More Than a Song

The sanctuary was quiet. A single guitar strummed softly in the background. The congregation swayed gently, eyes closed, arms raised. For many, this was worship—the moment when the lights dim, the music builds, and emotions swell. But is that all worship is? A slow song? A Sunday experience?

Worship is far more.

Worship is not bound to a melody, a mood, or a moment. It is not confined to a sanctuary, nor does it depend on the talent of a musician. It is, instead, a response to God's presence, His majesty, and His worth. Worship is not something we do to warm up before the sermon—it is the very reason we exist.

**Worship vs. Praise: The Difference That Matters**

The Bible speaks often of both praise and worship, but they are not identical. Praise is the celebration of who God is and what He has done. It is loud, joyful, and expressive. It's the shout of victory after a breakthrough, the song of deliverance after walking out of the fire.

Worship, however, is deeper. While praise often speaks of God's acts, worship responds to God's nature. It is reverent, quiet, intimate. Praise may precede worship, but worship brings you to your knees—sometimes literally. Praise is for everyone, but worship comes from a heart that has seen God and surrendered.

In Psalm 100:4, we are told to "enter His gates with thanksgiving, and His courts with praise." These are outer courts. But in the Holy of Holies, in that intimate place with God, it is worship that reigns. Worship is not merely the acknowledgment of God's greatness—it is the adoration of it.

**Biblical Definitions: Shachah and Proskuneo**

To truly understand worship, we must return to the original languages of Scripture. In Hebrew, the word most often used for worship is "shachah" (שָׁחָה), which means "to bow down, to prostrate oneself in reverence." It's not about volume or rhythm—it's about posture. A bowing of the body and soul in total submission.

In the New Testament, the Greek word is "proskuneo" (προσκυνέω), meaning "to kiss toward," as in the act of a servant bowing to kiss the feet or hand of a master. It evokes not only reverence but intimacy—a closeness that moves beyond admiration into deep love and surrender.

These two words—shachah and proskuneo—paint a portrait of worship that is not musical but relational. Worship is not about singing beautifully; it's about bowing truthfully.

**Worship as Surrender, Posture, and Intimacy**

Jesus' words to the Samaritan woman in John 4:23–24 were revolutionary. He said:

"Yet a time is coming and has now come when the true worshippers will worship the Father in the Spirit and in truth, for they are the kind of worshippers the Father seeks."

This was radical. In one sentence, Jesus redirected worship from a place to a posture—from a mountain or temple to a heart aligned with God. Worship, He said, must be in spirit (authentic, from deep within)

and in truth (anchored in who God is and who we are).
For Jesus, worship was not a religious performance; it was relational surrender.
Paul echoes this in Romans 12:1, saying:
"Therefore, I urge you, brothers and sisters, in view of God's mercy, to offer your bodies as a living sacrifice—holy and pleasing to God—this is your true and proper worship."
Here, Paul connects worship to sacrifice. Worship is laying down your life, your desires, your agenda. It is offering yourself not as a burnt offering on a physical altar, but as a living, breathing, willing vessel of God's glory. Worship is costly. But it is also liberating.

**A Farmer's Worship: The Story of Dev**
Dev Joshi, a 54-year-old wheat farmer from central India, knew nothing about guitars, choirs, or sound systems. His days were spent sowing seeds, inspecting the soil, and praying for rain. But every morning before sunrise, Dev would walk into his field, take off his shoes, and whisper, "This land belongs to You. I belong to You."
He never sang in public. But his neighbors noticed something strange. Even in years of drought, Dev's field remained green. When asked, he would smile and say, "The Lord walks with me here." What they didn't see was that every failure, every blessing, every decision was preceded by Dev's quiet act of worship—bowing in his heart before the Lord.
His worship was surrender and trust—a living example of shachah.

**A CEO's Worship: The Story of Simone**

Simone Turner, a high-powered executive in Chicago, once believed worship was something reserved for Sundays. During the week, she ran meetings, closed deals, and chased success. But everything changed after a health scare forced her into the hospital for weeks.

In her hospital bed, stripped of titles and influence, Simone met God in silence. There were no choirs, no lights—just her and Him. She remembered her grandmother's old song: "I need Thee every hour." She whispered it over and over. Slowly, her heart softened.

When she returned to work months later, Simone was different. She began each day by kneeling in her office. No one saw. She didn't post about it. But her leadership changed—more grace, more peace, more clarity. Her boardroom had become her altar. Her worship was intimacy and transformation—a daily proskuneo.

**A Teenager's Worship: The Story of Kemi**

Kemi Olanrewaju, a 17-year-old girl in Lagos, Nigeria, battled anxiety and low self-worth. At school, she felt invisible. At home, overlooked. One night, after a particularly bad day, she locked herself in her room and played a worship song on repeat: "You say I am loved when I can't feel a thing…"

She wept. Not just because of pain, but because for the first time, she believed that God saw her. She didn't know the theology of worship, but she knew how to be real. And that night, in the privacy of her room, she gave God her heart—her shame, her fears, her future.

That was worship. Pure. Honest. Surrendered.

**Worship Is a Life Aligned**

Worship is not limited by culture, language, or music. It is not reserved for a stage or a set list. Worship is the alignment of your entire life with the worthiness of God. It is bowing low so that He may be lifted high. It is not a performance—it's a posture.

Whether in the fields of India, the boardrooms of Chicago, or the bedrooms of Nigerian teens, worship breaks through every wall. It is the weapon of the surrendered. It is the fragrance of the faithful. It is the heartbeat of the heaven-bound.

*Worship is more than a song.*

*It is your life—bowed low before a worthy King.*

# Chapter 2: The Purpose of Worship

The early morning mist still hovered low over the hills as twelve-year-old Malakai Tsegaye crouched beside his grandmother's wooden stool. They sat outside their clay home in northern Ethiopia. She was humming a tune without words. "What are you singing, Nana?" Malakai asked. She smiled, eyes closed, voice low.

"I'm not singing," she whispered, "I'm worshipping."

That morning, Malakai learned something many never do their whole lives: worship is the reason we were made. Before we were teachers or doctors, before we were farmers or artists, before we were anything else—we were created to worship. It is not something we add to our lives; it is the center from which all life flows.

**Why God Created Us to Worship**

God, in His infinite wisdom and beauty, did not create humanity out of need. He lacked nothing. He was not lonely or bored. Within the Trinity—Father, Son, and Holy Spirit—was perfect fellowship, perfect joy. Yet, in the overflow of that divine love, God chose to create us. And He designed us with one primary purpose: to glorify Him and enjoy His presence forever.

In Isaiah 43:7, the Lord says,

*"Everyone who is called by My name, whom I created for My glory, whom I formed and made."*

Again, in Isaiah 43:21, He declares:

"*The people whom I formed for Myself that they might declare My praise."*

This is not narcissism. This is not a dictator demanding flattery. This is a Creator inviting His creation to live in the only posture that brings wholeness: worship. When we worship, we reflect His glory—like mirrors catching the light of the sun.

Worship aligns us to the very essence of our design. Just as a fish was made for water and a bird for the sky, so were we made for communion with God. And worship is the oxygen of that communion.

But worship is not simply for God's pleasure; it is for our transformation. It shapes us. It heals our identity. It reorders our affections. It lifts our gaze from what is temporary to what is eternal.

**Alignment with Divine Order**

Imagine a symphony where each instrument plays without a conductor. Chaos. Noise. But with the conductor's baton, order returns. Each sound finds its place. The music becomes not just notes but beauty.

So it is with worship. Worship restores divine order. It reminds us of who God is—sovereign, holy, glorious—and who we are—dependent, beloved, created. It corrects the spiritual disorder caused by pride, self-focus, and sin. In worship, God is enthroned in our hearts again, and all else falls into its rightful place.

When we fail to worship, we don't become neutral—we redirect that worship. Human beings are incurably worshipful creatures. If not God, we worship ourselves, money, success, comfort, celebrities, or ideology. The golden calves may look different today, but they are still idols. And idols always distort.

King David understood this deeply. In Psalm 29:2, he wrote:

*"Ascribe to the LORD the glory due His name; worship the LORD in the splendor of holiness."*

David didn't just worship in song; he restructured a kingdom around God's presence. He built tabernacles, appointed musicians, and centered governance around worship. Why? Because he knew worship was not an event—it was the engine of divine alignment.

**Worship in Heaven: A Glimpse into Glory**

If you could peek into heaven right now, what would you see?

John, the beloved disciple, gives us a glimpse in Revelation chapters 4 and 5. Transported into the throne room of God, John does not see confusion or silence—he sees unceasing worship. He describes it with awe:

"Day and night, they never stop saying: *'Holy, holy, holy is the Lord God Almighty, who was, and is, and is to come.'"* (Revelation 4:8)

Heaven is not preoccupied with earthly success or politics. Heaven is locked in continuous adoration. Around the throne are four living creatures, twenty-four elders, and myriads of angels. They cry out, not because they are told to, but because they cannot help it.

In Revelation 5, the scene escalates. The Lamb—Jesus—takes the scroll, and worship explodes: *"Worthy is the Lamb who was slain, to receive power and wealth and wisdom and might and honor and glory and blessing!"* (Revelation 5:12)

Heaven's worship is not passive. It is active, loud, filled with purpose and power. It is eternal, untainted by time or sin. Every act of true worship on earth is an echo of this heavenly reality.

When we worship here, we join the chorus there.

**The Sculptor's Awakening: The Story of Marco**

In Florence, Italy, Marco Delini spent thirty-five years shaping marble into beauty. An acclaimed sculptor, Marco created monuments for presidents, fountains for cities, and art for collectors. But inside, he felt empty. His hands worked, but his soul ached.

One autumn afternoon, he visited a small chapel on a whim. There, a priest read aloud from Revelation 5. As Marco listened to the cries of "Worthy is the Lamb," something cracked open in his heart.

Tears fell. For the first time, he realized he had worshipped his own gift instead of the Giver. He had used his creativity to build a name, not a throne.

That night, he sculpted differently. Not for buyers or applause—but as worship. Each stroke of his chisel became a prayer. His work became aligned with divine order—not centered on man, but on God. **His** worship was redemption.

**The Mother's Resilience: The Story of Nandita**

Nandita Paul, a 43-year-old single mother in Kolkata, raised three children on her own. Life was hard. Her hands bore the calluses of laundry washed by stone. Yet every evening, once her children were asleep, she would sit beside their bed, close her eyes, and whisper worship songs into the quiet.

She never went on stage. No spotlight ever found her. But heaven knew her voice.

One night, her daughter Meera asked, "Maa, why do you worship even when nothing changes?" Nandita smiled, tears in her eyes. "Because even when life is unfair, God is still good. And He is worthy."

That night, Meera joined her. Two voices. One candle. A heavenly chorus. Nandita's worship was not comfort-driven—it was kingdom-aligned. It brought peace into chaos, order into exhaustion. It was eternal perspective wrapped in daily struggle.

**The Tech Designer's Breakthrough: The Story of Dax**

In Seoul, South Korea, Dax Min, a software designer for one of the world's top tech companies, was known for his innovation. But he was also consumed by anxiety. Algorithms were his life—but he couldn't program peace.

One day, he attended a Christian retreat. A preacher read Revelation 4 aloud. Dax, used to code and logic, was stunned by the imagery—thrones, creatures, crowns, lightning, worship.

He scribbled in his journal: *"Heaven is ordered by worship. No fear. No striving. Just reverence. Maybe that's the missing piece."*

Returning home, Dax didn't quit his job—but he started each day in stillness, whispering worship before touching a keyboard. He redesigned his workspace with Scripture. Even his software became inspired by divine order.

His code flowed smoother. His mind calmed. His worship wasn't noise—it was submission.

**Worship Is Heaven's Purpose in Earthly Vessels**

Worship is not a church tradition—it is the very reason we were created. In worship, we align ourselves with heaven. We become part of the eternal narrative unfolding even now before the throne of God.

When we worship, we don't escape the world—we engage it from heaven's perspective. We realign. We recalibrate. We declare who is truly worthy.

Our purpose is not productivity or popularity. It is presence. To behold God. To adore Him. To magnify Him. Not because He needs it—but because we do.

So whether you are sculpting in Italy, scrubbing floors in India, or designing code in Seoul—worship.

*Because this is why you were made.*

*And this is where you find your true self—face to face with the One who sits on the throne.*

# Chapter 3: Why Worship is a Weapon

It was 3:14 a.m. in the city of Manila. Inside a small prayer room tucked between concrete tenements and neon-lit billboards, Ariana de Vega, a widowed nurse, sat with her hands lifted heavenward. Her youngest child had just been diagnosed with leukemia. The fear was suffocating. But as tears streamed down her face, something unexplainable happened. Peace arrived. Not because the diagnosis changed, but because worship shifted the battle.

Ariana didn't know it then, but she had just picked up one of the most powerful weapons in the spiritual realm.

**The Fall of Lucifer: The Origin of the Battle**

To understand why worship is a weapon, we must go back to the first rebellion, the first fracture in heaven's perfect harmony. That fracture didn't begin with man. It began with Lucifer—the first worshipper.

According to Ezekiel 28:12–17, Lucifer was not always the adversary. He was once "the seal of perfection, full of wisdom and perfect in beauty." He was adorned with every precious stone—sardius, topaz, emerald, sapphire. He was anointed as a guardian cherub. He walked among the fiery stones, dwelling in the very courts of God.

But there was something else: he was crafted for worship.

*"The workmanship of your timbrels and pipes was prepared for you on the day you were created"* (Ezekiel 28:13).

Music flowed through him. Praise emanated from his being. But then something shifted.
Isaiah 14:13–14 unveils the core of Lucifer's fall:
*"You said in your heart: 'I will ascend to the heavens; I will raise my throne above the stars of God… I will make myself like the Most High.'"*
Lucifer wanted worship not to give, but to receive. The created desired to be exalted above the Creator. The mirror meant to reflect glory became a black hole, sucking it in.
And thus, the first war began—not with swords, but with worship.
Lucifer was cast out, becoming Satan, the adversary. But he never stopped craving worship. And he never stopped trying to steal it.

**Why Satan Targets Worship**
When Jesus was led into the wilderness, Satan tempted Him with many things. But notice the climax in Matthew 4:9:
*"All these I will give you," he said, "if you will bow down and worship me."*
He didn't ask for a sermon. He didn't ask for loyalty. He asked for worship.
Why?
Because Satan knows what many believers forget: worship determines allegiance. Whatever you worship, you surrender to. And whatever you surrender to, you serve.
That is why Satan's ultimate tactic is to redirect worship—from God to self, from spirit to flesh, from eternal to temporary. He uses fame, ego, comfort, and even fear to seduce our worship.

But when a believer, even in the pit of despair, chooses to lift their hands and exalt God, hell trembles. Worship becomes warfare.

**Worship Dethrones Self and Enthrones God**

At the heart of all spiritual battles is this question: Who sits on the throne of your heart?

Worship is the declaration that it is not me. Not my preferences, my plans, my pain, or my pride. Worship dethrones self and enthrones God. It is the lifting of His name above all others.

The apostle Paul writes in Romans 12:1:

*"Present your bodies as a living sacrifice, holy and acceptable to God, which is your spiritual worship."*

This is not poetic metaphor. This is a call to battle—to offer everything to God, not on our terms but on His.

Every time we worship, we tear down the idols of self. Every hallelujah says, *"You reign, not me."* Every *"Holy, holy, holy"* is a sword through pride. Worship is the daily act of surrendering the throne to the rightful King.

**Worship Changes the Atmosphere and Silences Fear**

In Psalm 8:2, David declares:

*"From the lips of children and infants you have ordained praise to silence the enemy and the avenger."*

Praise silences the enemy. It mutes his lies. It dismantles fear.

When Paul and Silas were locked in a prison in Acts 16, they didn't strategize an escape plan. They sang hymns at midnight. And the prison shook. Chains fell. Doors opened. Not because of sound decibels, but

because worship shifted the spiritual atmosphere.
Worship invites heaven into earth's problems. It rewrites fear with faith. It takes our focus off the storm and fixes it on the Storm-Calmer.
As Paul later writes in Romans 12:2:
*"Do not conform to the pattern of this world, but be transformed by the renewing of your mind."*
Worship renews. It aligns our thoughts with truth. It tunes our spirits to heaven's frequency.

**The Soldier's Secret: The Story of Kwame**
**Kwame Nyarko**, a Ghanaian army officer, was deployed in a violent border conflict. Surrounded by hostility, he watched fellow soldiers collapse under fear and PTSD. But Kwame carried something different.
Every night, he opened a small notebook filled with Scriptures and worship lyrics. He'd hum softly—"Way Maker, Miracle Worker..."—beneath the stars. His platoon called him "The Singing Shield."
One night during an ambush, chaos erupted. But Kwame fell to his knees, lifted his hands, and began to sing Psalm 23 aloud. The enemy retreated inexplicably. Bullets missed. Fear melted.
Kwame didn't win the battle through tactics. He won it through worship. Worship was his secret weapon.

**The CEO's Turning Point: The Story of Gloria**
Gloria Tamas, a high-powered CEO in Toronto, ruled boardrooms with efficiency—but she was losing her soul. Panic attacks. Insomnia. Fear of losing control.
One Sunday, she reluctantly walked into a small church on a friend's invitation. During the worship, the worship leader began singing:
*"I'm no longer a slave to fear, I am a child of God."*

Tears welled up. She couldn't explain it. She hadn't cried in years.
For the first time, Gloria laid down control. She lifted her hands and whispered, *"Jesus, I surrender."* Peace flooded in.
From that day, worship became her morning ritual—not yoga, not espresso, but adoration. Her boardroom decisions improved. Her fear vanished. She had finally dethroned herself.

**The Abandoned Child's Refuge: The Story of Elias**

Ten-year-old Elias Garza, abandoned in a Brazilian favela, had only a torn Bible and his grandmother's songs in memory. He would climb the rooftop every night and sing.
He didn't know all the words. But he'd say, *"Jesus, I love You. You're my Papa."*
In a world that rejected him, worship made him feel seen. It was his refuge, his protection, his identity.
Years later, Elias became a worship pastor. But he never forgot those rooftop nights. He says, *"Worship kept me alive. Not because it changed the world around me—but because it changed me."*

**Worship Wins Wars**

Worship is not passive. It is a weapon forged in heaven.
It dismantles pride. It dethrones idols. It realigns our hearts. It silences demons. It rebuilds faith.
It does what nothing else can—bring heaven to earth.
The next time fear whispers, or chaos reigns, or temptation comes knocking—don't just
fight. Worship.

Because when you worship, you do what Satan can't—and what he hates.
You remind him of what he lost.
And you remind yourself of who still reigns.
*You may not have swords. You may not have strength.*
*But if you have a song of surrender,*
*you have already won.*

# Chapter 4:
# Warfare in the Spirit Realm

It was just past dawn in Lagos, Nigeria. Adeyemi Olabode, a schoolteacher by profession and intercessor by conviction, stood on the roof of his modest home, staring out over the slums where his students lived. That morning, he wasn't praying for finances or a promotion. He was battling for the soul of his city.

His hands trembled, not from fear, but from a deep, pulsing awareness of what he could not see but could deeply sense—a war raging in the unseen. And like a seasoned soldier, Adeyemi knew this: you don't bring knives to a gunfight—and you don't fight spiritual battles with earthly tools.

**Defining Spiritual Warfare (Ephesians 6:12)**

To understand warfare in the spirit realm, we must first see the invisible. The apostle Paul opens our eyes in Ephesians 6:12:

*"For we wrestle not against flesh and blood, but against principalities, against powers, against the rulers of the darkness of this world, against spiritual wickedness in high places."*

This is not poetic language. It is military. The word "wrestle" suggests close combat. This isn't sniper warfare from a distance. It's hand-to-hand. It's personal.

Paul identifies our enemies—not people, but principalities (territorial spirits), powers (forces that influence decisions), and rulers of darkness (systems and ideologies shaped by evil). These are not fairy

tales or metaphors. These are real spiritual entities operating behind human systems.
If we attempt to fight with carnal arguments, manipulation, or anger, we lose before we begin. But if we put on the armor of God and understand our true weapons, we engage on the battlefield where victory has already been declared.

**The Weapons of Warfare: Worship, Word, Prayer, Fasting**

Paul continues in 2 Corinthians 10:4:
*"For the weapons of our warfare are not carnal but mighty in God for pulling down strongholds."*
What are these weapons? The Word, prayer, fasting—and worship.

**The Word of God**

The Word is our sword (Ephesians 6:17). Not a decorative one. A sword meant to be wielded. Jesus used it in the wilderness when tempted by Satan, declaring, *"It is written..."* (Matthew 4:4). The Word is not just for comfort—it's for combat. Every verse is a missile against lies. Every declaration is a blow to deception.

**Prayer**

Prayer is not merely asking—it is legislating. It is inviting heaven's authority into earth's crisis. It is declaring war on darkness in secret and watching God move in public. The prophet Daniel's intercessory prayer in Daniel 10 led to angelic intervention and revealed the spiritual resistance in Persia.
Prayer is not a fallback. It is an airstrike.

**Fasting**

Fasting is the stripping away of the flesh to sharpen the spirit. Jesus said in Matthew 17:21, *"This kind does not go out except by prayer and fasting."* Fasting weakens the influence of carnal desires and makes room for divine power. It empties us so God can fill us.

But there is one weapon that often gets underestimated…

**Worship's Unique Role Among Spiritual Weapons**

Worship is not just a prelude to the sermon. It is battle strategy. When done in spirit and truth, worship is explosive in the spirit realm.

Jehoshaphat understood this in 2 Chronicles 20. When Judah was surrounded by three vast armies, Jehoshaphat didn't consult his generals first. He consulted the Lord. God's battle plan?

*"You will not need to fight in this battle. Stand still and see the salvation of the Lord"* (2 Chronicles 20:17).

And then, the unexpected happened:

*"He appointed those who should sing to the Lord, and who should praise the beauty of holiness, as they went out before the army saying: 'Praise the Lord, for His mercy endures forever'"* (v.21).

As they worshipped, the Lord ambushed their enemies. Not by military tactics—but by confusing their enemies into turning on each other.

Worship disorients the enemy and aligns the spirit realm with God's dominion.

**When Worship Shifts the War: The Story of Leila**

Leila Santiago, a 43-year-old Chilean single mother and call center supervisor, discovered this truth during the most painful year of her life. Her son Mateo was falsely accused of drug possession and

imprisoned. Her church fasted, her lawyer fought, but the case remained frozen in bureaucracy.
One night, after weeping in her car for hours, Leila went home and turned off the lights. She lit a single candle and began to sing an old hymn in Spanish, "Grande es Tu fidelidad..." (Great is Thy faithfulness).
She sang it over and over. Then switched to declaring Psalm 27 aloud:
*"Though an army encamp against me, my heart shall not fear..."*
What she didn't know was that at the exact hour she worshipped, a junior prosecutor was led to review Mateo's file and noticed an inconsistency that exonerated him.
Two weeks later, Mateo walked free.
Leila wasn't just surviving. She was warring. With worship.

**The Tension of Two Worlds: The Story of Neil and the Boardroom**

In London, Neil Ford, a sharp-minded investment banker, was fighting a different kind of war. His firm had been infiltrated by greed and moral compromise. Whistleblowers were silenced. Neil knew the pressure to either comply or be crushed.
But Neil did something rare for someone in a pinstripe suit. Each morning before entering the glass towers of Canary Wharf, he'd lock himself in his car and worship.
No music. Just whispered songs like "Be Still My Soul" and Psalm 91.
At a critical shareholders meeting, Neil exposed fraudulent accounting with boldness. He expected backlash, even termination.

But instead, upper management cleared house, and Neil was promoted.

Worship had prepared him for war. It gave him courage to confront darkness in a suit and tie.

### Worship as Heaven's Language

What makes worship different from other weapons is that it originates in heaven. The Word teaches us. Prayer connects us. Fasting sharpens us. But worship is the language of eternity.

In Revelation 5:11-12, we glimpse into the throne room:

*"Then I looked, and I heard the voice of many angels… saying with a loud voice: 'Worthy is the Lamb who was slain…'"*

Heaven is not busy strategizing. It is worshipping. That's the position of ultimate authority—unbroken adoration.

When we worship, we join heaven's anthem. And because Satan once stood in that throne room as a lead worshipper, he knows what it sounds like. Worship reminds him of everything he lost, and every time we lift our voices, we declare that he has already been defeated.

### Conclusion: The Battle Belongs to the Lord, But We Must Sing

The war is real. The enemies are unseen. But the outcome is certain.

When you worship, you align your spirit with the victory already won at the cross. You aren't begging God for help. You are declaring the triumph of the risen Christ over every demon, every lie, every threat.

As you stand in battle—whether in the boardroom like Neil, the slums like Adeyemi, or the prison waiting room like Leila—remember this:
You are not powerless. You are not weaponless.
Worship is your warfare. The name of Jesus is your anthem.
And victory is your destiny.
*So raise your voice—not after the breakthrough, but before it.*
*Because worship doesn't just celebrate victory.*
*Worship causes* it.

# PART II:
# BIBLICAL WARFARE THROUGH WORSHIP

# Chapter 5: Worship in the Old Testament – Power and Deliverance

Long before there were cathedrals or choirs, before microphones and musical instruments filled auditoriums, there was a sound that shook the heavens—a sound not refined by music theory but birthed from obedience, desperation, and faith.

It was the sound of worship, and in the Old Testament, this sound became a weapon, a shield, and a declaration of deliverance.

From the dusty roads of Jericho to the throne room of Saul, worship was not ornamental—it was operational. It summoned divine presence, routed enemies, and brought peace to tormented minds. Worship was, and still is, God's battle strategy.

**The Fall of Jericho's Walls (Joshua 6)**

The first biblical war Israel fought after entering the Promised Land wasn't won by spears or chariots. It was won by obedient worship.

In Joshua 6, God gave Joshua a seemingly illogical command: march around the fortified city of Jericho once a day for six days in complete silence. On the seventh day, march around it seven times, then have the priests blow the trumpets and the people shout.

It was not a battle cry born out of adrenaline but a shout born from trust in the unseen Commander.

*"So the people shouted when the priests blew the trumpets... and the wall fell down flat..."* (Joshua 6:20)

This was not magic. It was worship in obedience. A sound that aligned with heaven's timing.

**Nandini's Wall of Debt**

Thousands of years later, in the city of Hyderabad, Nandini Rao, a widowed garment worker, was drowning in generational debt. Every month, creditors knocked harder. She couldn't read English well, but a friend gave her a Telugu Bible and pointed her to Joshua 6.

Nandini couldn't afford legal help or bank intervention. But every night for seven nights, she walked around her tiny one-room home, holding her toddler, whispering praise songs and declaring, *"The walls will fall."*

On the eighth day, she got a call from a local Christian NGO that had received funding to cancel debt for struggling women—and she was on the list.

She collapsed to her knees, singing a broken but pure melody of praise. Her Jericho had fallen. Not through strength, but through worship.

**Jehoshaphat's Victory (2 Chronicles 20)**

Years after Joshua, another king—Jehoshaphat—faced an alliance of armies too great for Judah to defeat. His natural instinct might have been to rally the military. But Jehoshaphat sought the Lord through fasting and prayer.

God's answer came not through tactics, but through worship.

*"You shall not need to fight in this battle. Position yourselves, stand still and see the salvation of the Lord..."* (2 Chronicles 20:17)

And what did Jehoshaphat do? He sent worshippers ahead of the army, singing, *"Praise the Lord, for His mercy endures forever!"* (v. 21).
As they worshipped, the Lord caused confusion among their enemies. The enemies turned on each other and were completely destroyed.
Victory was secured before swords were drawn—because worship had gone before them.

**Diego's Unexpected Strategy**
In São Paulo, Brazil, Diego Morales, a youth pastor and part-time mechanic, faced a crisis of his own. His church had been wrongly sued over a zoning violation, and the entire building was set to be seized. The congregation panicked. Some wanted to protest; others wanted to go silent.
But Diego recalled Jehoshaphat's story. On the morning of the court hearing, he gathered the youth and worship team in the church courtyard. As the city stirred around them, they lifted up voices in Portuguese: *"Senhor, Tua misericórdia dura para sempre…" (Lord, Your mercy endures forever).*
The judge who had been handling their case had a sudden personal emergency, and a new judge was assigned—one who was favorable toward churches and quickly dismissed the false charges.
As Diego worshipped, God warred on his behalf. It didn't make the headlines, but in the spirit realm, it was a battlefield soaked in song.

**David's Harp and Saul's Deliverance (1 Samuel 16:23)**
Worship does not only break down walls and confuse enemies—it restores minds tormented by darkness.

King Saul was a man tormented by an evil spirit. His advisors sought relief, and they found it in the form of a young shepherd boy named David, who played the harp with divine favor.

*"And so it was, whenever the spirit from God was upon Saul, that David would take a harp and play it with his hand. Then Saul would become refreshed and well, and the distressing spirit would depart from him."* (1 Samuel 16:23)

It wasn't the notes that brought deliverance—it was the spirit behind the sound, the anointing born in fields of private worship.

**Tyler's Battle of the Mind**

In Detroit, Tyler Benson, a former U.S. Marine struggling with PTSD, found himself paralyzed by anxiety and night terrors. Years of therapy had helped, but nothing could touch the deep spiritual oppression he felt when night fell.

One day, he stumbled into a small church where a young girl played soft worship music on the piano. Tyler sat in the back, weeping as *"It Is Well with My Soul"* echoed through the sanctuary.

That night, he slept peacefully for the first time in months.

He started returning regularly, often just sitting in the sanctuary while worship filled the room. Slowly, the torment began to lift—not because of a sermon, but because of the harp of David echoing through a 21st-century piano.

Worship, then and now, still brings deliverance to tormented souls.

**The Tabernacle of David and Continuous Worship (Psalm 22:3)**

King David, the same young man who soothed Saul, later established something revolutionary: the Tabernacle of David, a tent where worship was offered to God day and night, continually (1 Chronicles 16).

Psalm 22:3 reveals the foundation of this worship:

*"But You are holy, enthroned in the praises of Israel."*

David understood something eternal—God doesn't just inhabit buildings; He inhabits praise. Continuous worship meant continuous enthronement. Where praise is, God sits as King.

**Grace's Garden Tent**

In the rural fields of Ghana, Grace Ankomah, a retired midwife, turned her gardening shed into a place of praise. Every morning and every night, she played worship songs, read the Psalms aloud, and sang while tending her hibiscus flowers.

Neighbors mocked her at first, calling her "the mad singing widow." But over time, troubled youth began stopping by her garden. Some were suicidal. Some were lost. But something in that shed—a tangible peace—drew them in.

Soon, her home became known as the "House of Rest."

Unknowingly, Grace had built her own Tabernacle of David, and as worship filled the air, God made her garden His throne.

**Worship Is Ancient, Yet Present**

From the rubble of Jericho to the hills of Ghana, from David's harp to Diego's youth choir, worship in the Old Testament was not an accessory—it was an

arsenal. It brought walls down, scattered armies, calmed tormented kings, and established God's rule among people.
What worked then still works now. Because the God who received worship from David's harp is the same God who moves through every sincere voice raised in reverent praise today.
So let us remember: When we worship, we don't just honor history—we join it. We step into the lineage of spiritual warriors who conquered not by sword or strategy but by song and surrender.
*Worship is power.*
*Worship is deliverance.*
*Worship is warfare.*

# Chapter 6:
# Worship in the New Testament – Power and Breakthrough

Worship in the New Testament is not merely a continuation of the Old; it is its consummation and transformation. In the life, death, and resurrection of Jesus Christ, worship is no longer confined to location or ceremony but becomes a way of life, a rhythm of power, and a channel of breakthrough.
Where the Old Testament laid the foundation, the New Testament unveils the fullness—worship that transcends prison walls, confronts agony, fills homes and hearts, and thunders through heaven itself.

**Paul and Silas in Prison (Acts 16:25–26)**
It was midnight. The hour when most dreams fade and darkness feels its heaviest. Paul and Silas had been beaten, chained, and thrown into the inner cell of a Philippian prison—not for wrongdoing, but for casting out a spirit of divination.
Their bodies were bruised, their feet bound. And yet, they worshipped.
*"About midnight Paul and Silas were praying and singing hymns to God, and the other prisoners were listening to them."* (Acts 16:25)
They didn't sing because they were free. They sang because they knew freedom was not determined by chains but by presence. Worship turned that prison into a sanctuary. And heaven responded.
*"Suddenly there was a great earthquake, so that the foundations of the prison were shaken; and*

*immediately all the doors were opened and everyone's bonds were unfastened."* (v. 26)
God didn't just shake the physical structure—He loosed every bond.

**Ava's Breakthrough Behind Bars**
In a correctional facility in Manila, Ava Dela Cruz, a former drug mule, sat on the cold concrete floor of her cell. She had come to Christ through a prison chaplain's Bible study, but shame clung to her like a second skin.
One night, feeling especially broken, she whispered a melody her grandmother used to sing over her:
*"Ama, Ikaw ang kanlungan ko..." (Father, You are my refuge...)*
Her cellmate joined in. Then another. Within minutes, five women were humming the hymn. The guards heard it but didn't stop them. Something sacred hovered in the air.
That night, Ava had a dream of chains melting. Two weeks later, her sentence was unexpectedly reduced due to new evidence. But deeper than legal mercy was this: Ava had worshipped her way into freedom long before the court did.

**Jesus in Gethsemane (Matthew 26:30)**
As Jesus prepared for the cross, His soul was sorrowful to the point of death. But before heading to Gethsemane, He shared the Passover meal with His disciples. And then, remarkably:
*"And when they had sung a hymn, they went out to the Mount of Olives."* (Matthew 26:30)
Think about that. The Son of God, knowing He would be betrayed, tried, tortured, and crucified, sang a hymn.

Worship in this moment wasn't about celebration—it was about surrender. In singing, Jesus acknowledged the sovereignty of the Father and chose to obey unto death. Worship became His posture in pain.

**Kofi's Cup of Suffering**

In Accra, Ghana, Kofi Mensah, a street evangelist, had just received news that his youngest son had died from a sudden illness. His knees buckled in the hospital corridor.

Later that night, sitting on the veranda of his small home, Kofi couldn't find words to pray. But a hymn rose in his spirit: *"When peace like a river attendeth my way..."*

Tears fell, but he sang anyway. As he sang, he felt the Lord whisper, *"Even in the garden, I sang."*

Kofi realized that worship in grief isn't denial—it's divine alignment. In his darkest hour, Jesus sang. And in Kofi's Gethsemane, worship became his will's surrender.

**The Early Church: Songs, Hymns, and Spiritual Songs (Ephesians 5:19)**

As the early church formed its identity in a hostile world, worship became a lifeline. The Apostle Paul wrote:

*"Speaking to one another with psalms and hymns and spiritual songs, singing and making melody in your heart to the Lord."* (Ephesians 5:19)

Worship in the early church was not entertainment. It was edification. It was spiritual warfare disguised as melody. It infused courage into persecuted hearts and unity into diverse gatherings.

These songs were truth wrapped in tune. They reminded slaves of their dignity, widows of their worth, and new believers of their new birth.

### Elena and the Underground Church

In a small village in North Korea, Elena, a 62-year-old believer, met secretly with five others in a root cellar lit by a single candle. Bibles were forbidden, so they had memorized entire passages.

Their worship was silent—only mouths moving without sound. But in their hearts, they sang:

*"Christ alone, Cornerstone, weak made strong in the Savior's love…"*

Each meeting ended with humming—a soundless harmony of faith. When one of their group was arrested, the others didn't scatter. Instead, they returned the next night, whispering Psalm 46:1:

*"God is our refuge and strength, a very present help in trouble."*

To Elena, worship wasn't an act. It was oxygen.

### Heaven's Worship in Revelation (Revelation 5, 19)

If there is any doubt about the power of worship, the book of Revelation clears it. Worship is not just for earth—it is the language of eternity.

*"Then I looked, and I heard the voice of many angels around the throne… and the number of them was ten thousand times ten thousand… saying with a loud voice: 'Worthy is the Lamb who was slain…'"* (Revelation 5:11–12)

Heaven is not silent. It resounds with unceasing worship. From the elders casting their crowns to the multitudes proclaiming His worth, the throne of God is surrounded by song.

In Revelation 19, as judgment is completed and the bride is ready, a thunderous voice cries:
*"'Alleluia! For the Lord God Omnipotent reigns!'"* (Revelation 19:6)
This is the endgame: unbroken worship in the presence of the King.

**Zara's Vision of Glory**
In rural Canada, Zara McLeod, a retired nurse battling cancer, spent her final months in hospice. Her daughter would often play worship music quietly beside her bed.
One night, Zara opened her eyes and whispered, *"Do you hear them singing?"*
*"What do you mean, Mom?"* her daughter asked.
Zara smiled, tears rolling down her face. *"They're singing, 'Worthy is the Lamb.'"*
She passed away moments later.
Her daughter realized what many miss: for those who know Christ, death is not the end—it is the doorway into worship without end.

**Worship is the Key to Breakthrough**
From the prison cell to the olive grove, from candlelit basements to celestial realms, the New Testament reveals that worship is not bound by circumstance.
*It is a song in suffering.*
*A sword in the spirit.*
*A surrender in the storm.*
*And a seal of the saints.*
Paul and Silas used it to break chains. Jesus embraced it to endure the cross. The early church used it to build one another up. And heaven never stops declaring it.

We are part of that same worship stream. When we raise our voices—not for applause, but from adoration—we join with angels and apostles, martyrs and missionaries, shepherds and slaves.
*Worship is our breakthrough.*
*Worship is our battle cry.*
*Worship is our home.*

# PART III:
# THE WORSHIPPER'S HEART
## Character & Consecration

# Chapter 7: The Heart of a Worship Warrior

True worship is not the product of performance or presentation—it is the fruit of the heart. A worshipper may play no instrument, stand on no platform, and carry no microphone, yet still wage war in the heavenlies if their heart is postured right before God. The strength of a worship warrior does not lie in vocal range or musical ability, but in brokenness, surrender, humility, and intimacy.

At its core, worship is a heart posture—one of dependence, obedience, and devotion. It is not simply about what we do during a worship session, but who we are before God. Before there is power in our praise, there must be purity in our hearts.

**Brokenness, Surrender, and Humility**

The worshipper's strength begins in brokenness—not despairing brokenness, but holy brokenness, the kind that acknowledges, *"Without You, Lord, I am nothing."*

In Psalm 51:17, King David—having been confronted with his sin with Bathsheba—offered one of the most profound revelations of acceptable worship:

*"The sacrifices of God are a broken spirit, a broken and a contrite heart—These, O God, You will not despise."*

David understood that no burnt offering could substitute for a heart crushed by the weight of conviction and longing for restoration. Brokenness doesn't repel God; it draws Him near.

**Caleb's Cry**

Caleb Owusu was a worship leader in Kumasi, Ghana. Charismatic and talented, he drew crowds to the church every Sunday. But over time, pride crept in like smoke. He started to gauge success by applause, views, and reactions on social media.

Then one evening, during rehearsal, he lost his voice. Days turned into weeks. Doctors found no cause. His confidence shattered. Alone in his room, he broke before God, weeping, not for his voice, but for his heart that had gone astray.

He remembered Psalm 51 and whispered, *"Create in me a clean heart, O God..."*

That night, he didn't sing. He worshipped—with silence, tears, repentance, and surrender. His voice returned eventually, but it no longer carried just melody—it carried weight. From that day, Caleb sang from brokenness, not performance.

**Worship in Spirit and Truth (John 4:24)**

Jesus, in His conversation with the Samaritan woman at the well, unveiled a radical truth:

*"God is Spirit, and those who worship Him must worship in spirit and truth."* (John 4:24)

True worship is not bound by location, race, ritual, or style. It must flow from the spirit—the deepest part of our being—and be aligned with truth—God's nature and His Word.

Worship in spirit means it is alive, intimate, and God-breathed. Worship in truth means it is anchored in who God really is, not who we imagine Him to be.

**Mei's Meeting at the Well**

In the outskirts of Taipei, Taiwan, Mei-Ling Tsai had grown up in a home filled with Buddhist tradition. In university, she met Christ through a quiet classmate who loved the Word. Mei struggled at first—Christianity felt foreign, Western, and rigid.

One day while reading John 4, Mei came across the phrase *"worship in spirit and truth."* Something clicked.

She whispered, *"Lord, I want that. Not religion, not ritual—realness."*

Alone in her dorm room, she put down her notes, lifted her hands, and said, *"I don't know how to worship like others. But I give You my heart."*

Tears streamed. Her first worship song wasn't in English or even Mandarin. It was the sound of truth meeting spirit, of a heart unlocking to divine presence.

From that moment, Mei became a quiet pillar in her church—never on stage, but always hosting His presence. She had learned that worship wasn't about fitting in—it was about being genuine before God.

**Intimacy Before Intercession**

Many want to be powerful in prayer, effective in intercession, or bold in the prophetic. But before any of these, the worship warrior must first learn intimacy. Worship precedes warfare. Friendship with God is the foundation of fruitfulness in the kingdom.

Moses, before becoming a leader of Israel, was a friend of God who met with Him face to face (Exodus 33:11). The power of Moses' leadership flowed from the tent of meeting, not the palace of Pharaoh.

Mary of Bethany offers a New Testament parallel. While Martha busied herself with service, Mary chose to sit at Jesus' feet—to listen, adore, and behold.

*"Mary has chosen the good portion, which will not be taken away from her."* (Luke 10:42)

Intimacy is the good portion—the heart's true home.

**Jared's Tent of Meeting**

In the small town of Clearwater, Texas, Jared Whitaker was a high school teacher by profession and a quiet intercessor by calling. He longed to see revival in his city but often felt unseen and unheard.

Each morning at 5:00 a.m., before school, he would sit in the attic of his old farmhouse with his Bible and a guitar. No soundproofing. No spotlight. Just coffee, candlelight, and communion with God.

Sometimes he'd sing softly. Other times he'd just whisper, *"I love You."*

Years later, a powerful youth revival broke out in his school. Students gathered for prayer, repented, and turned to Christ. When asked what started it, one of the students said, *"There's something about Mr. Whitaker's class—it feels like peace walks in with him."*

They didn't know. But heaven knew. Intercession was born in intimacy. Jared's attic had become his tent of meeting. His worship was his warfare.

**The Inner Altar Must Burn**

The heart of a worship warrior is not made in public places—it is formed in secret ones. It is not a product of charisma but consecration. These warriors carry no visible armor, but they wear the fragrance of brokenness, truth, and intimacy.

They are the Davids before the Goliaths, the Marys before the service, the Pauls before the praise.

God is still seeking such worshippers—not perfect ones, but postured ones. Hearts bowed low. Hands lifted high. Souls set aflame.

If you desire to become a true worshipper, start not with a song, but with a surrender. Let your life be the melody, your spirit the sanctuary, and your love the offering.

*For in the Kingdom, the greatest warriors do not always roar.*

*Sometimes, they weep.*

*Sometimes, they whisper.*

*Always, they worship.*

# Chapter 8: The Enemies Worship Confronts

Worship is not just a song—it is warfare. When a believer enters into true worship, they step into the frontlines of a spiritual battlefield. But unlike traditional warfare fought with metal and muscle, the enemies of worship are not merely external. They often lie hidden within us or operate subtly in the atmosphere around us. Worship, in its purest form, is confrontational. It exposes and overthrows that which resists the Lordship of Christ—in our hearts and in our environments.

True worship isn't comfortable. It will confront the flesh, drive out fear, expose darkness, and silence the false gods of pride, distraction, performance, apathy, and idolatry. These enemies must be brought low before the throne of God, where true worship lifts Him high.

**Worship Confronts the Flesh (Romans 8:5–8)**

The flesh is our fallen nature—the part of us that resists the Spirit, craves control, and centers self. Paul writes in Romans 8:7, *"The mind governed by the flesh is hostile to God; it does not submit to God's law, nor can it do so."* Worship confronts the flesh by demanding surrender. Where the flesh says "me," worship declares "You."

When we worship, we dethrone ourselves. The desires of the flesh—pride, anger, lust, laziness—are suffocated under the weight of divine glory. You cannot truly worship and remain in agreement with your sinful nature.

**Raul's Fight to Let Go**

Raul Fernandez was a young entrepreneur in São Paulo. Ambitious and sharp, he had built a successful tech startup by the age of 27. He was also a Christian—nominally. Sunday mornings were a routine, but his heart was anchored to his business more than his God.

One morning during worship, the worship leader began singing, *"I surrender all."* Raul stood still, arms folded. A quiet whisper stirred in his spirit: *"Do you really?"*

He left that service shaken. That night, alone in his apartment, Raul wrestled with God. He saw how his flesh—the desire to be admired, secure, in control—was sitting on the throne of his heart.

Tears fell as he knelt and said, "*Jesus, I step down. You take over.*"

From that night forward, Raul didn't just attend worship—he engaged it. He learned to let the Spirit rule over the flesh. Worship became his daily practice of surrender.

**Worship Confronts Fear (2 Timothy 1:7)**

Fear thrives in the absence of faith and the absence of focus on God. But worship recalibrates our gaze. When we lift our eyes from our problems to our Provider, fear begins to dissolve.

Paul reminded Timothy, *"For God has not given us a spirit of fear, but of power, and of love, and of a sound mind."* (2 Tim. 1:7). Worship is the act of refusing to let fear have the final word. It is the voice of faith singing in the face of what feels uncertain or impossible.

**Jaya's Night of Peace**

In the busy city of Mumbai, Jaya Iyer was a nurse working long shifts during a sudden dengue outbreak. One evening, overwhelmed and afraid of catching the virus herself, she sat alone in her hostel room, paralyzed by anxiety.

Her Bible lay untouched on her shelf. But that night, unable to sleep, she picked it up and read Psalm 27:1: *"The Lord is my light and my salvation—whom shall I fear?"*

In the quiet, she began to hum an old worship song her mother used to sing: *"Because He lives, I can face tomorrow..."* That small melody became her lifeline. Worship pushed back the darkness that fear had erected in her mind.

The circumstances hadn't changed, but her spirit had. Worship became her defiant weapon of peace.

**Worship Confronts Darkness (Psalm 149:6–9)**

There is something explosive about worship when it rises in the face of evil. Psalm 149 says, *"May the praise of God be in their mouths and a double-edged sword in their hands..."* Worship is not passive—it is militant. It proclaims God's dominion and pushes back demonic resistance.

Satan cannot tolerate an atmosphere of worship because it dethrones him. Where God is lifted up, darkness must flee.

**Isaac's Midnight Hour**

In a rural village in Kenya, Isaac Njoroge, a widower and father of three, faced ongoing spiritual oppression. Strange things occurred at night—his children had night terrors, and his home felt heavy.

He met an older pastor who gently told him, *"Your home needs praise, not just prayers."*

That night, Isaac gathered his children and began to softly sing Psalm 91. By the third night, something shifted. The fear lifted. Peace entered. Darkness had been driven out—not by volume, but by victory-saturated worship.

Isaac's house became a house of praise, and demonic patterns were broken through consistent exaltation of God's name.

**Worship Confronts Pride, Distraction, Performance, Apathy, and Idolatry**

These subtle enemies often camouflage themselves as good things—success, service, even ministry. But when unchecked, they rob God of the honor He alone deserves.

- ✓ Pride says *"I'm enough."*
- ✓ Distraction says *"God, I'll get to You later."*
- ✓ Performance says *"Let me impress You."*
- ✓ Apathy says *"It doesn't matter."*
- ✓ Idolatry says *"You're not enough—I need more."*

Worship, in Spirit and truth, confronts all of them.

**Lena's Wake-Up Call**

Lena Kovacs was a celebrated worship artist in Budapest. Her calendar was full, her fan base growing, but her heart was dry. One afternoon, at a youth event, the power went out just before her set. No lights, no sound.

Instead of cancelling, the youth pastor asked, *"Can we just sit before the Lord?"*

For 45 minutes, silence filled the room—then spontaneous singing. No leader. No chords. Just hearts crying out.

Lena sat weeping. She realized how much she had been performing, not communing. She had made ministry her idol, and distraction her default. That night, she rededicated her heart not just to music, but to worship.

The next album she released was called *"Undone."* It wasn't her bestselling, but it was her most anointed—because it came from a heart purified by confrontation with the living God.

**The Battle Begins Within**

Worship is not always loud or pretty, but it is always powerful. And before it shakes the heavens, it must first shake us. It exposes enemies within: the flesh, fear, pride. It drives out enemies without: darkness, distraction, idolatry. Every time we truly worship, something false has to bow.

God is not looking for flawless voices, but for surrendered hearts. When we worship, the King is enthroned, and every other pretender to the throne is unmasked and undone.

So next time you raise your hands or bow your knees in worship, know this:

*You are confronting more than you realize.*

*You are not just singing.*

*You are warring.*

# Chapter 9: Worship in the Midst of Trials – The Sacrifice of Praise

There is a kind of worship that does not rise from abundance or comfort, but from ashes. It is not clothed in joy, but soaked in tears. It does not come from a place of answers, but from a posture of raw trust. This is the sacrifice of praise—worship offered in the middle of trial, pain, and uncertainty. It is the most costly worship of all, because it is given when everything in you wants to shut down, withdraw, or curse God.

In the moments when the heart is crushed and the soul feels abandoned, to lift our eyes and say *"Blessed be Your Name"* becomes a declaration of deep faith, not shallow optimism. It is not pretending all is well—it is proclaiming God is still worthy even when all is not well.

The Bible is not unfamiliar with suffering. From Job to the prophets, from Paul to Jesus Himself, Scripture gives voice to groans, grief, and lament—but also to unrelenting worship in the midst of it all. This is the heartbeat of the sacrificial praise that honors God most.

**Worship When It Hurts (Job 1:20–21)**

Job, a man described as *"blameless and upright,"* lost almost everything in a single day—his children, his wealth, his servants, his stability. The news came in like crashing waves. Any lesser man might have collapsed in bitterness. But Job's response pierces the soul:

*"Then Job arose and tore his robe and shaved his head, and he fell to the ground and worshiped. And he said: 'Naked I came from my mother's womb, and naked I shall return. The Lord gave, and the Lord has taken away; blessed be the name of the Lord.'"* (Job 1:20–21, ESV)

He didn't worship after he healed. He didn't worship after God restored him. Job worshipped in the dark, when all he had left was a broken heart and a fragile hope. This is the essence of sacrificial praise.

**Amira's Midnight Cry**

In a small town near Cairo, Amira Youssef, a devoted schoolteacher and single mother, lost her son Kareem in a tragic accident. Her world shattered in a moment. The days that followed were filled with a pain that words couldn't hold.

On the seventh night, she sat in Kareem's room, clinging to his sweater, unable to sleep or eat. The grief clawed at her chest. In the stillness, a song from her childhood rose unbidden in her spirit:

*"You give and take away… My heart will choose to say, Lord, blessed be Your Name…"*

She didn't sing it loudly—just a whisper between sobs. But that whisper was a roar in heaven. It was praise not based on outcome, but on allegiance. Amira didn't praise because she understood—she praised because she still trusted.

In that moment, heaven drew close. The sacrifice of praise turned her room into an altar, and she became a worshipper not of comfort, but of covenant.

**The Theology of Lament**

Lament is not weakness. It is not faithlessness. It is the biblical language of sorrow directed toward God, not away from Him. The Psalms are full of it—David cried, *"How long, Lord? Will You forget me forever?"* (Psalm 13:1). Jeremiah wept over Jerusalem. Even Jesus lamented with loud cries in Gethsemane and on the cross.

Lament is not complaining—it is communion in pain. It acknowledges grief but still engages God. Lament is how worship continues when answers do not come.

**Dawit's Broken Hallelujah**

In the highlands of Ethiopia, Dawit Mengesha was a worship leader in a small rural church. One year, locusts devoured the region's crops, and his entire community faced famine. His family lost their land, and his wife fell gravely ill.

Dawit tried to pray, but no words came. One morning, he opened his Bible to Lamentations and read, *"Yet this I call to mind and therefore I have hope: Because of the Lord's great love we are not consumed"* (Lamentations 3:21–22).

He picked up his battered guitar and began to sing—not songs of victory, but songs of *presence*. "*You are here… even in this wilderness."* He sang through tears, not triumph. His lament was sacred—it told the truth of the pain and the goodness of God.

Dawit's worship became the anchor of his village. People who had no food still gathered to sing, and joy slowly returned—not because life was easy, but because God had not left.

**Hebrews 13:15 and Rejoicing in Suffering (Romans 5:3–5)**

Hebrews 13:15 calls believers to *"offer to God a sacrifice of praise—the fruit of lips that openly profess his name."* A sacrifice implies cost. Praise is

easy when blessings flow. But when life is breaking, and worship still rises? That is sacred.
Paul adds in Romans 5:3–5 that we rejoice in our sufferings, not because suffering is good in itself, but because it produces perseverance, character, and hope—a hope that does not disappoint because God's love is poured into us.
Sacrificial praise isn't denial. It's defiance—declaring that God's goodness outranks our grief.
**Jonas' Fire and the Song That Remained**
In the cool hills of Bavaria, Jonas Kessler, a young pastor, watched his small church building burn down after an electrical fire. Years of effort, sacrifice, and community building went up in smoke in a single night.
The next morning, standing among ashes, he gathered the congregation in the open field next to the ruins. People looked on with sadness and despair. Jonas opened his Bible and quietly read, *"Rejoice in the Lord always. Again, I say rejoice."* (Philippians 4:4)
He began to sing—not a grand anthem, but a simple chorus:
*"I will bless the Lord at all times… His praise shall continually be in my mouth."*
As voices joined, a holy wind swept across that field. Mourning turned to courage. Praise became the rebuild. The building was gone—but the fire of worship burned hotter than ever.

**When Praise Costs Something**
The sacrifice of praise is the song sung in pain, the hallelujah whispered through tears, the hands raised though empty. It is not always eloquent or musically

perfect. But it is pure. It carries the fragrance of surrender and the sound of true faith.

When we worship in trials, we are not ignoring our suffering—we are reframing it. We are saying*: "This storm doesn't define me. This pain doesn't have the final word. God does."*

Heaven sees these moments. They echo louder than choirs. They strike chords that resonate in eternity.

*So when it hurts, worship anyway. When it doesn't make sense, lift your voice. When you feel like giving up, give God a sacrifice.*

*Because praise in the valley is the worship that moves mountains.*

# Chapter 10:
# Worship as a Daily Lifestyle

Worship was never meant to be confined to cathedrals or constrained to Sunday mornings. It is not a song service, nor is it simply a genre of music. Worship is a way of life—a constant outpouring of devotion, obedience, and love for God in the ordinary rhythm of everyday existence.

Jesus never said, *"Worship the Father once a week."* He said, "Worship in spirit and truth." (John 4:24) That kind of worship transcends platforms and pulpits—it flows through breakfast tables, office desks, traffic jams, and late-night hospital corridors. A true worshipper carries an inner sanctuary, a heart always tuned to heaven's frequency.

## Worship at Work, at Home, in the Car, and in the Chaos

It is not hard to worship in a peaceful sanctuary. But what about when you're folding laundry? Meeting tight deadlines at the office? Stuck in city traffic? God is no less present in these places.

Worship becomes real when it spills over into the mundane moments—when your heart bends in reverence while cooking dinner, when your thoughts drift toward gratitude while driving, when your soul offers silent praise between conference calls. These are the living sacrifices of Romans 12:1—*"Offer your bodies as a living sacrifice, holy and pleasing to God—this is your true and proper worship."*

### Rafael's Commute

Rafael Mendoza, a logistics manager in Manila, begins his day before the sun rises. His commute through Manila's crowded streets often stretches to two hours. But instead of frustration, Rafael has turned his car into a chapel.

With worship music softly playing and his hands on the wheel, he begins his mornings not with complaints but with communion. He prays aloud over his family, blesses his workplace, and sometimes just remains in silence, listening for God's whisper.

Once, during a particularly stressful season at work involving layoffs, he found peace only during these car rides. *"God, this car is my altar,"* he often said. *"I meet You here."* That daily devotion didn't change his circumstances immediately—but it changed him, giving him wisdom, peace, and unusual joy even in uncertainty.

**Holy Habits: Prayer, Scripture, Solitude, Silence**

Worship becomes a lifestyle when it is **anchored in habits** that make space for God. Jesus Himself modeled this. He withdrew often to quiet places, prayed alone at night, quoted Scripture constantly, and kept His heart tuned to the Father.

These holy habits are not legalistic boxes to tick—they are lifelines that tether us to the divine. Prayer speaks. Scripture feeds. Solitude clears the noise. Silence listens.

**Naomi's Corner of Grace**

In the bustling city of Lagos, Naomi Adeyemi, a widowed grandmother raising two grandchildren, created a sacred rhythm amidst her chaos. Every morning at 5:30 a.m., before the children stirred, she would pour herself a cup of tea, open her worn Bible, and sit quietly by the window.

She called it her *"Corner of Grace."* No fanfare. No loud declarations. Just steady communion.

When one of her grandsons was falsely accused in school, Naomi didn't react in anger. She returned to her corner, wept before God, and prayed. Later that week, the truth came to light.

Her grandchildren grew up not only knowing Bible stories but witnessing a living altar in their grandmother's daily life. Worship was not just in what Naomi sang—it was in what she practiced.

**Creating Private Altars (Matthew 6:6)**

Jesus said, *"When you pray, go into your room, close the door and pray to your Father, who is unseen. Then your Father, who sees what is done in secret, will reward you."* (Matthew 6:6)

This private place—be it a literal room, a chair in the corner, a park bench, or even a quiet closet—is not about geography. It is about intentional intimacy. It is where you meet God without an audience. Where performance dies, and authenticity is born.

Private altars shape public lives. A worshipper who kneels in private will walk upright in public.

**Caleb's Closet**

Caleb Anders, a former marine turned high school coach in rural North Dakota, wasn't known as a man of many words. But behind his stoic exterior was a life of private worship.

Years ago, during a battle with alcoholism, he cried out to God in desperation. That night, he cleared out the hall closet in his apartment, put down a pillow, and began to kneel there every evening. He read the Psalms. He journaled. He worshipped in the dark.

Even after finding healing and sobriety, Caleb never stopped going to that closet. It became his holy ground. And though his players only saw the discipline, integrity, and strength in him—they never knew it was forged in a sacred closet of surrender.

When one of his students was diagnosed with cancer, Caleb visited the boy every week. And in his quiet way, he would always say, *"I'm praying for you, son. Every night. In my closet."* The boy's parents later said that comforted their child more than anything else.

**A Life of Worship is a Life Fully Alive**

Worship as a lifestyle is not about perfection. It is about posture. It is a heart perpetually bowed before God, whether on the mountaintop or in the valley, whether holding a guitar or holding a grocery list.

It is the daily decision to see God in everything—in chores, in traffic, in spreadsheets, in laughter, in tears. It is singing in the shower and praying while sweeping the floor. It is whispering *"Thank You"* for breath and boldly declaring "*You are worthy*" when nothing goes your way.

Such worship transforms us. It tunes our hearts to eternity, reshapes our desires, and marks our days with joy, peace, and power. And the beauty of it? It doesn't require a stage—just a heart willing to see every moment as sacred.

**Final Reflection**

Where is your altar?

Maybe it's not a room. Maybe it's a park trail, a kitchen table, a seat on the train. Wherever it is, let it become a place where your spirit meets the Spirit of God—daily, honestly, quietly.

*Let your whole life sing.*

# PART IV:
# WORSHIP AS STRATEGIC SPIRITUAL WARFARE

# Chapter 11:
# Strategic Worship for the Battle

Worship is not merely an expression of affection; it is a weapon of war. It is not simply the atmosphere before the sermon—it is the strategy of heaven released on earth. In the unseen realm, where principalities and powers rage against the children of God, worship becomes more than music. It becomes militant.

When we worship, we are not retreating—we are advancing. We are not avoiding the battle—we are confronting it. True worship is never passive; it is a spiritual stance. It confuses the enemy, disarms the demonic, and releases divine power. Scripture is filled with moments where worship preceded victory, where praise went before power, and where songs broke strongholds.

**Offensive vs Defensive Worship**

There is a difference between worship that reacts and worship that initiates. Defensive worship is often birthed in the storm—it cries out for rescue, it pleads for strength, it shields the soul. But offensive worship is what sets the terms of engagement. It steps out in faith *before* the breakthrough, declaring the victory already won in Christ.

In 2 Chronicles 20, Jehoshaphat didn't wait for the enemy to retreat before worshipping. He sent worshippers ahead of the army, declaring, *"Give thanks to the Lord, for His love endures forever."* (2 Chronicles 20:21) That was offensive worship. And the moment they began to sing and praise, the Lord set ambushes against their enemies.

**Karabo's Advance**

Karabo Ndlovu, a young schoolteacher in Pretoria, South Africa, understood this principle not through a seminary, but through suffering. After being falsely accused by a colleague of misconduct, Karabo was placed on indefinite suspension. The shame crushed her spirit, and her name was nearly ruined.

One night, while in deep anguish, she remembered the story of Jehoshaphat. She turned off her phone, walked into her living room, and lifted her hands. "You are my defender, Lord," she whispered. "And You are worthy even if no one else believes me." Then she began to sing—not songs of desperation, but songs of confidence in God's justice.

Every day for the next three weeks, Karabo would worship before sunrise—not asking for vindication, but declaring who God was. On the twenty-third day, the charges were dropped. The accuser confessed. Karabo returned to school, not only cleared but spiritually matured. Her worship had been warfare, and God had fought for her.

**Scriptural Declarations in Worship**

Worship is not emotional hype—it is often grounded in truth that is declared. The Word of God, when combined with the spirit of worship, becomes a two-edged sword in the believer's hand. (Hebrews 4:12)

In Psalm 149, the psalmist writes: *"Let the high praises of God be in their mouths and a double-edged sword in their hands, to inflict vengeance on the nations and punishment on the peoples..."* (Psalm 149:6–7)

There is power in singing the Scriptures, in declaring His promises aloud in the presence of opposition. When Jesus was tempted by Satan in the wilderness, He didn't reason or argue. He declared, *"It is written..."* (Matthew 4:4). When those words are mingled with praise, they shake the unseen world.

**Isaac's Victory Room**

Isaac Delgado, a former gang member turned pastor in Los Angeles, created what he called a "Victory Room" in the back of his small house. The walls were lined with sticky notes filled with Scriptures—every promise, every prophecy, every decree that had been spoken over his life.

Each morning, Isaac would step into the room, turn on worship music, and begin pacing back and forth, declaring Scripture out loud as he worshipped. When his teenage son was caught in gang trouble, Isaac went to his Victory Room and declared Psalm 91 over him, again and again.

When financial troubles hit the church, he didn't send fundraising emails—he worshipped with Psalm 23 on his lips. His congregation began to follow his example, and soon testimonies of breakthrough started flooding in.

One woman said, *"It was the first church I attended where worship was more than music—it was how we fought our battles."*

**Intercession Through Praise and Worship**

Worship is not always about what God is doing for us—sometimes it's about contending for what God wants to do through us on behalf of others. This is intercessory worship—when praise becomes a cry for mercy, a declaration over someone else's valley, a shield for someone else's storm.

Paul instructs believers in Ephesians 6 to take up the full armor of God, and part of that armor is *"praying in the Spirit on all occasions with all kinds of prayers and requests."* (Ephesians 6:18). Worship can become such prayer—*melodic intercession*, reaching into nations, families, and wounded souls.

**Eliana's Sound of Rescue**

In the mountainous region of Cusco, Peru, Eliana Vargas, a quiet woman in her sixties, spent her life caring for abandoned children. Though she had no formal theological training, she had the heart of an intercessor and the voice of an angel.

Each night after putting the children to bed, Eliana would sit on the porch, look toward the mountains, and begin to worship. Her songs were soft, sung in Quechua, and always filled with pleas for protection and healing—not for herself, but for every child in her care.

Once, when a cholera outbreak swept the nearby villages, many children fell ill. Eliana turned her porch into a sanctuary. Neighbors would hear her singing deep into the night, crying out in song. *"Lord, cover these children with Your wings."*

Not one of the children in her home died.

Later, the village priest said, *"I believe it was Eliana's songs that kept death away. She fought the sickness with worship."* Her voice was her warfare. Her songs were intercession.

**Worship Is a Battle Plan**

Strategic worship is not about manipulating God—it is about aligning with heaven's perspective. It is declaring truth louder than lies, singing promises louder than problems, and raising praise louder than panic.

Worship shifts atmospheres. It awakens angels. It shakes prisons. It silences fear. And more importantly, it changes us, the worshippers, into warriors.

When the enemy attacks, let worship be your first response—not your last resort. When the battlefield stretches before you, lift your hands—not in surrender to the enemy, but in surrender to the King who has already won the war.

**Reflection**

- ✓ Do you view worship as warfare, or just as a moment of inspiration?
- ✓ What battles are you facing today that could be confronted with offensive worship?
- ✓ Can you begin incorporating Scripture into your daily praise?

Perhaps today is the day to build your own "Victory Room"—not with walls and nails, but with faith and declarations.

As the song says, *"This is how I fight my battles."* Worship is not weakness—it is warfare soaked in reverence, powerful because it is birthed in truth.

# Chapter 12:
# Prophetic & Apostolic Worship

Worship, in its purest form, is not limited to melodies and harmonies. It is a supernatural transaction between heaven and earth. At its highest levels, it becomes prophetic—declaring what is in God's heart—and apostolic—establishing His will and order in the earth.

Prophetic and apostolic worship is marked by spiritual authority, divine alignment, and heaven's vocabulary. It is when worship breaks beyond the natural and begins to speak, sing, and shape the future. In this dimension, the people of God are not merely offering praise—they are partnering with the Holy Spirit to release God's purposes in a place, a people, or a nation.

**Singing the Word and Declaring God's Names**

When we sing the Word of God, we are not reciting poetry—we are releasing power. Scripture is not a suggestion; it is divine decree, and when declared in worship, it brings clarity, healing, and deliverance. The Psalms are full of sung Scripture. David did not simply write theology; he sang revelation.

*"Sing to the Lord, bless His name; proclaim the good news of His salvation from day to day."* (Psalm 96:2)

Prophetic worship often includes the declaration of God's names—Yahweh, Elohim, El Shaddai, Jehovah Rapha, Jehovah Nissi, and others. Each name reveals a facet of His character. When we declare His names in worship, we are naming His presence over our situation—inviting His nature to reign.

### Anaya's Song of Names

Anaya George, a worship leader in the Caribbean island of St. Lucia, wasn't always prophetic in her worship. For years, she simply led with the latest popular songs. But in the wake of a devastating hurricane, when homes were flooded and her own church was torn apart, she was left with no instruments, no sound system, and no power.

One Sunday, she stood under the tin-roofed remains of their sanctuary with only a handful of people and no music. As she looked at the sky, she whispered, "Lord, what do I sing when there is nothing left?"

A still, small voice replied: *"Sing My names."*

So she began slowly: *"You are Jehovah Jireh, my Provider. You are Jehovah Rapha, my Healer. You are Jehovah Shalom, my Peace."* As the names of God filled the space, something shifted. People wept. Healing began. Joy returned. Anaya learned that the most prophetic worship is not new—it is eternal.

She would later testify, *"The day I sang His names was the day the storm ended—not outside, but inside us."*

### Spiritual Authority in Worship

Prophetic and apostolic worship is rooted in spiritual authority. This authority is not loudness or style—it comes from intimacy with God, obedience to His voice, and alignment with His will.

Jesus exercised spiritual authority not through performance, but through position—He was rooted in the Father. When He spoke, the wind and waves obeyed (Mark 4:39). When He prayed, the dead rose. That same spiritual authority is extended to His followers—not for fame, but for Kingdom establishment.

**Martin's Fire on the Floor**

Martin Liu, a quiet custodian in Beijing, never imagined himself as someone with spiritual authority. But every morning before anyone entered the underground church where he worked, Martin would kneel in the sanctuary and sing softly to the Lord. No one saw him. No one knew. But heaven listened.

One morning, as government officials threatened to shut down the church, fear gripped the congregation. But that Sunday, as Martin quietly began to sing the words of Isaiah 54—*"No weapon formed against you shall prosper..."*—a tangible fire of the Spirit fell.

Without a microphone, his voice echoed through the basement. Elders wept. Youth fell to their knees. The government agents who came that week left confused and never returned. Something unseen had shifted.

Martin wasn't a leader by title—but in the spirit realm, his worship carried weight. Because authority in worship isn't about who holds the mic—it's about who walks with God.

**Sounds of Heaven and Warfare (Psalm 150)**

Psalm 150 paints a powerful picture of heaven's sound:

*"Praise Him with the sound of the trumpet… with the harp and lyre… with tambourine and dancing… with strings and pipe… with loud cymbals… with resounding cymbals."* (Psalm 150:3–5)

This is not a quiet, reserved moment. It is a war cry. It's the sound of heaven's armies marching. In heaven, worship is thunderous, victorious, and alive. When believers tap into this dimension on earth, their worship becomes a replica of heaven's atmosphere.

Prophetic worship releases these heavenly sounds. Sometimes they come through instruments, sometimes through spontaneous songs, sometimes through holy silence. But they always do one thing—they tear through darkness and announce the rule of God.

**Samuel's Sound of Deliverance**

In Nigeria, Samuel Bamidele was a young boy when his village was attacked by armed militants. As bullets rang through the air, his mother grabbed his hand and ran to the church at the hilltop. Many villagers huddled together in fear, sobbing and crying.

But Samuel's mother, a former choir leader, stood up and began to beat a small drum. She started to sing—loud, bold, unshaken: *"Let God arise and His enemies be scattered..."*

The song caught fire. Others joined in. The worship grew louder than the fear. Something powerful broke through the atmosphere. That night, the militants withdrew. No one could explain it.

Later, one of the village elders said, *"It was like they heard something greater than us—some sound from above."*

Samuel would grow up to lead worship movements across Africa. He often said, *"Worship is not noise. It's a heavenly invasion."*

**Worship That Establishes and Releases**

Prophetic and apostolic worship is not a style. It is a function. It declares, it releases, it breaks, it builds. It doesn't simply entertain; it establishes God's dominion.

In prophetic worship, the Word becomes a sword. In apostolic worship, the Spirit builds foundations.

Together, they usher in divine order, healing, deliverance, and justice. The Church must move beyond stage-driven performances and rediscover the sacred, strategic place of singing the Word, declaring His name, and releasing the sound of heaven.

This kind of worship changes cities. It shifts regions. It pulls down strongholds. It silences devils. It lifts Jesus up—and when He is lifted, *He draws all people to Himself* (John 12:32).

**Reflection**

- ✓ Are you singing songs, or are you declaring truths in worship?
- ✓ Are you using your voice to release the names of God into your atmosphere?
- ✓ What would happen if your worship aligned more closely with heaven's sound?

Perhaps today is the day to open your Bible during worship—not just your mouth—and begin to sing the Word. Declare Jehovah Nissi over your battles. Declare El Shaddai over your weakness. And watch as the weight of heaven meets the sound of your praise.

# Chapter 13:
# Worship That Breaks Strongholds

Worship is not only a song—it is a sledgehammer in the spirit. It is God's tool to tear down what has been fortified by lies, fear, trauma, and sin. Strongholds are not just demonic infestations in dark corners—they are *patterns of thinking*, *cycles of bondage*, and *generational chains* that keep hearts from fully walking in the freedom Jesus paid for.

But worship changes that. True worship exposes lies and enthrones truth. It reclaims territory lost to the enemy. It brings the soul into alignment with God's voice. In worship, we trade despair for hope, curses for blessing, torment for peace, and addiction for deliverance. Worship is not a retreat from battle—it is often the *final blow* that brings breakthrough.

**Worship and Deliverance**

Throughout Scripture, we see worship not just as expression, but as exorcism. In *1 Samuel 16:23*, when Saul was tormented by a distressing spirit, it wasn't a sword or a priest that drove it out—it was David's harp.

*"And so it was, whenever the spirit from God was upon Saul, that David would take a harp and play it with his hand. Then Saul would become refreshed and well, and the distressing spirit would depart from him."* (1 Samuel 16:23)

David didn't rebuke the spirit. He worshipped. And the presence of God filled the room so fully that darkness could not remain.

**Jordan's Breakthrough in the Basement**

In Chicago, Jordan Wells, a 33-year-old former drug dealer, had spent years in and out of rehab. Every time he got clean, the nightmares returned—of the violence, the abandonment, the guilt. One night, at the church where he was now volunteering, Jordan wandered into the basement after a Bible study.

The worship team had left their keyboard behind. No one was around. He touched the keys and began to play the one song he remembered from childhood: *"Jesus, Jesus, how I trust Him…"*

As he sang, something inside began to break—grief, shame, fear. For nearly an hour, Jordan wept and sang, repeating Jesus' name again and again. The torment lifted. Not temporarily—permanently.

That night, Jordan was delivered. No altar call. No laying on of hands. Just Jesus. Just worship. Just freedom.

**Breaking Generational Chains**

Strongholds often root themselves in generations—curses passed down through trauma, addiction, unforgiveness, or occultism. But God is a chain-breaker, and worship is one of His chosen tools.

In *Acts 16:25–26*, Paul and Silas worshipped in prison, and *not only were their chains broken, but "everyone's chains were loosed."* (v. 26). True worship doesn't just set *you* free—it ripples outward to those around you and even to those who came before you.

**Leticia's Lineage**

Leticia Duarte, a Brazilian mother of two, had come from a long line of spiritualism and witchcraft. Her grandmother was a well-known medium, and her mother often practiced rituals in the house. Leticia grew up terrified of the spirit world.

As a new Christian, she struggled with fear and demonic dreams. But her church introduced her to worship not just as music, but as a spiritual weapon.

One day, as she played a worship playlist while cleaning, the words of a song gripped her: *"I am a child of God—I'm no longer a slave to fear."* She stopped everything, raised her hands, and began declaring the lyrics aloud.

Suddenly, a deep cry erupted from within her. She fell to her knees and began to name the fear, the rituals, the generational curses that had bound her family.

From that day on, her house felt different. Her children slept peacefully. The nightmares stopped. And two years later, her mother—once a practicing spiritist—accepted Christ and was baptized.

Leticia's worship didn't just cleanse her home. It cleansed **her family line**.

**Overcoming Temptation and Oppression Through Adoration**

Strongholds aren't always visible. Sometimes they show up as addictions of the heart—jealousy, lust, comparison, anger. Sometimes they come as temptation, hitting when you least expect it. But the presence of God, accessed through worship, becomes a *shield* and a *sword*.

When Jesus was tempted in the wilderness, He didn't sing, but He declared truth. Yet right before His arrest—when temptation pressed on His humanity in Gethsemane—He sang a hymn with His disciples. (Matthew 26:30)

In His greatest moment of testing, He chose to worship.

**Asha's Secret Struggle**

Asha Bedi, a 24-year-old accountant in New Delhi, was a youth leader by day and a prisoner of hidden shame by night. She battled a quiet but relentless addiction to online pornography—something no one knew about.

She prayed. She fasted. She wept. But the shame kept her from truly drawing near to God.

One evening, in desperation, she shut her laptop, turned on her phone's worship playlist, and lay face down on her bed. The song playing was *"Here I am to worship, here I am to bow down…"*

She whispered, "God, I don't even feel worthy to sing this. But I need You more than I need to hide."

Something broke.

Every night after that, instead of fighting the temptation in silence, she began worshipping through it—declaring her identity, exalting Jesus, and speaking Scripture over herself.

The addiction didn't vanish overnight, but the stronghold lost its grip, because worship had enthroned Christ where secrecy and shame once ruled.

Today, Asha counsels other young women through similar battles, leading with this simple truth: *"You don't fight temptation by resisting harder—you fight it by adoring deeper."*

**Worship Destroys What Binds**

Strongholds thrive in silence, shame, and secrecy. They feed off lies, generational agreements, and personal wounds. But when worship enters, truth resounds, and truth always makes people free.

Whether torment, addiction, curses, or internal sin patterns—no chain can resist the sound of surrendered adoration.

Worship is not just a weapon. It is a wrecking ball. It demolishes the walls we didn't build but still live behind. It tears down high places where idols were once exalted. It unearths the foundations of fear and drives out the darkness that has overstayed its welcome.

*Let the music play.*

*Let the Word be sung.*

*Let your voice rise—even trembling and broken.*

*Because when a worshipper opens their mouth in faith, the heavens open, the ground shakes, and strongholds fall.*

# PART V:

# TRAINING TO BECOME A WORSHIP WARRIOR

# Chapter 14:
# A 30-Day Practical Action Plan

Worship isn't merely an act—it is a discipline. And like any soldier preparing for battle, a worship warrior must train daily, develop holy habits, and learn how to remain spiritually awake in every season. This 30-day action plan is not about perfection but about posture. It is not a checklist but a calling. You are being invited into a deeper, richer, and more powerful relationship with God where worship is not an occasional song—but a way of life.

This plan is built over four weeks, each designed to help you move from building the altar **to** becoming the altar—a living, breathing vessel of worship that shifts atmospheres, tears down strongholds, and hosts the presence of God daily.

## Week 1:
## Building the Altar

*"Then Elijah said to all the people, 'Come near to me.' So all the people came near to him. And he repaired the altar of the LORD that was broken down."* – 1 Kings 18:30

Every true worship journey begins at the altar—not necessarily a wooden platform, but the inner place of surrender where sacrifice is laid and fire falls. Before you can offer worship that transforms, you must repair what's been broken, restore intimacy, and clear the debris of distraction.

**Leila's Renewal**

Leila Anoma, a 42-year-old government clerk in Uganda, had grown numb in her faith. Busy with raising three children and working overtime, worship had become a Sunday event—not a daily breath. One morning, during a power outage, she lit a candle and sat quietly at her kitchen table. She whispered a simple prayer: *"God, here I am again. I'm tired, but I want You."*

For seven days, Leila began to rise an hour earlier—no phone, no noise—just silence, Scripture, and her own trembling voice singing softly. On the third morning, she wept uncontrollably. Not from sadness—but from the overwhelming presence of God that flooded her small kitchen.

By the end of the week, she said, *"I didn't find God in a church service. I found Him at my kitchen table—when I made space for Him again."*

In this first week, your goal is simple:

Clear your heart. Rebuild the altar. Reignite the flame.

- ✓ Set a dedicated time and space for daily worship.
- ✓ Begin each day with repentance and thanksgiving.
- ✓ Invite God to inspect your heart and remove what hinders connection.

## Week 2:
## Practicing His Presence

*"Evening and morning and at noon I will pray, and cry aloud, and He shall hear my voice."* – Psalm 55:17

Worship is not a once-a-day appointment; it's an all-day awareness. Practicing His presence is about being attentive to God in the mundane—in your commute, while folding laundry, during your lunch break. It's the sacred art of turning every moment into a sanctuary.

**Darius' Awakening**

Darius Chen, a 29-year-old software engineer in Singapore, was passionate about theology but disconnected from intimacy with God. After listening to a podcast on "practicing presence," he decided to structure his day around three sacred pauses: morning, mid-day, and evening worship.

Each morning before work, he read one Psalm aloud and sang a short chorus. At lunch, he stepped away from his desk, closed his eyes, and whispered declarations of God's faithfulness. At night, he played instrumental worship as he journaled.

After a week, he wrote in his journal: *"I used to believe I needed to feel goosebumps to know God was near. Now, I feel Him in my breath—in my boredom—in my silence."*

Practicing His presence is not about feeling—it's about faithfulness. God rewards those who seek Him with consistency, not just intensity.

## Week 3:
## Worship in Warfare

*"Let the high praises of God be in their mouth, and a two-edged sword in their hand..."* – Psalm 149:6

A worship warrior must be equipped to battle not only for personal freedom but for others. This week is about engaging in strategic worship—declaring God's Word aloud, crafting spiritual playlists, and fighting through praise. Praise is not the absence of problems; it is the defiant sound that declares: *"My God reigns in the middle of them."*

**Ruth and the Storm**

Ruth Langdon, a 37-year-old single mother in Birmingham, UK, found herself at war. Her son had been wrongfully accused in school, her job was at risk, and fear began to paralyze her. But instead of spiraling, she began crafting what she called her "Warfare Worship Kit."

Each morning, she would sing *"This is how I fight my battles"* while pacing her hallway. She printed out verses like *Romans 8:31*, *Isaiah 54:17*, and 2 *Chronicles 20:15*, taping them to her mirror. She played worship in the car, sang over her children, and declared Psalm 91 aloud daily.

A month later, her son was exonerated, her job was stabilized, and more than that—she was transformed.

Ruth later said, *"I didn't wait for the enemy to leave—I worshipped him out."*

This week, build your own warfare plan:

- ✓ Choose songs that focus on God's victory, power, and dominion.
- ✓ Write or speak personalized Scripture declarations daily.
- ✓ Intercede in worship for your family, your city, your church, and the nations.

## Week 4:
## Lifestyle of Worship

*"Therefore, I urge you, brothers and sisters, in view of God's mercy, to offer your bodies as a living sacrifice…"* – Romans 12:1

Worship that remains private never fully fulfills its purpose. True worship always spills out—into service, into community, into testimony. The final week is about activation. You are no longer just rebuilding—you are becoming a beacon, a witness, and a carrier of God's presence to others.

**Emmanuel's Overflow**

Emmanuel Durosinmi, a Nigerian university student studying in Canada, felt the nudge to begin leading worship in his dorm hallway on Friday nights. It began with just him and his guitar. By week three, three others joined. By week five, 20 students were gathered—many of whom had never attended church.

What started as a personal discipline became a public altar.

He said, *"God filled me so completely during those 30 days, I couldn't keep Him to myself. Worship became a fire I had to share."*

Your worship is not only for you. This week:

- ✓ Share a testimony publicly—online or in conversation.
- ✓ Organize a family or small-group worship night.
- ✓ Serve someone intentionally as an act of worship.
- ✓ Reflect each night on how your life is becoming an offering.

**Reflection, Journaling & Weekly Actions**

At the end of each week, take time to reflect with these prompts:

**Week 1 – Building the Altar**

- ✓ What needed to be cleared from your heart?
- ✓ Where did you experience God unexpectedly?

**Week 2 – Practicing His Presence**

- ✓ What surprised you about meeting God throughout your day?
- ✓ In what mundane space did you feel His nearness most?

**Week 3 – Worship in Warfare**

- ✓ What battles have begun to shift as you've worshipped?
- ✓ What Scriptures have become your spiritual weapons?

**Week 4 – Lifestyle of Worship**

- ✓ How has your worship impacted others this week?
- ✓ Where is God calling you to become a public altar?

Keep a journal through this journey. Track the transformation. Record dreams, verses, impressions. God is not just visiting you—He is training you. You are no longer simply a worshipper.

*You are now a Worship Warrior.*

# Chapter 15: Breakthrough Through Worship

There is something profoundly powerful about hearing the stories of those who have walked through the fire and emerged with songs on their lips. Worship is more than a melody—it is a weapon, a shelter, and sometimes a lifeline. It doesn't always change the situation immediately, but it always changes the worshipper. This chapter holds sacred space for the testimonies of individuals who discovered that worship wasn't just for Sunday mornings—it was the bridge between despair and deliverance, grief and glory, bondage and breakthrough.

As Psalm 40:3 declares, *"He put a new song in my mouth, a hymn of praise to our God. Many will see and fear the Lord and put their trust in him."* These are their songs.

**A Song in the Shadows: Grief and Worship**

Julianne Perera, a 47-year-old schoolteacher in Colombo, Sri Lanka, had always led her family's morning devotions, singing softly in the kitchen before her children awoke. But everything changed when her eldest daughter, Naomi, died in a tragic bus accident on her way to university.

For weeks, Julianne couldn't sing. Her lips were silent, and her soul numb. One evening, she stumbled upon Psalm 34:18: *"The Lord is close to the brokenhearted and saves those who are crushed in spirit."* With trembling hands, she reached for her guitar—untouched since the funeral—and whispered

an old hymn her grandmother had taught her: *"Abide with Me."*
As she sang through tears, something broke—not the pain, but the silence between her and God. The melody became her prayer, and her grief turned into a sacrifice of praise.
Months later, Julianne started a support group for grieving mothers called *Songs in the Shadows*. Together, they sing psalms of lament and worship, finding comfort in shared sorrow and shared song. Worship didn't erase her grief—but it became the lantern that lit her way through the darkness.
Just as David worshipped in the wilderness while being hunted by Saul (Psalm 57), Julianne learned to sing from a cave—and discovered that the cave can echo with heaven's songs.

**Healed in His Presence: Sickness and Worship**
Mikhail Orlova, a 34-year-old warehouse supervisor in St. Petersburg, Russia, had been diagnosed with an aggressive form of stomach cancer. He had no church background, no knowledge of worship, and no strength left in his body. One day, while waiting for a chemotherapy session, he overheard a young nurse humming *"How Great is Our God."*
He asked her what the song was, and she replied, *"It's a song of healing."* She offered to pray for him. Mikhail didn't object. Over the next few weeks, she would bring him recordings of worship songs in Russian, and Mikhail began to listen during his treatments.
He reported something unusual—when the music played, his nausea subsided. He felt a calm he couldn't explain. Eventually, he joined a small home

church and began singing softly with them. His body remained frail, but his soul was becoming vibrant.
Months later, his scans showed the cancer had stopped spreading. While he still continued medical care, Mikhail's faith had taken root. One Sunday, he led worship with shaking hands and a raspy voice. But the power in the room was undeniable.
Much like Hezekiah, who turned to the wall and worshipped when death loomed (Isaiah 38), Mikhail discovered that worship is not just for the healthy—it is for the hopeful. Healing may begin in the body, but it often starts in the spirit.

**Chains Broken: Addiction and Worship**

Tamara Jennings, a 28-year-old former heroin addict from Atlanta, Georgia, had lived through seven rehab centers, four overdoses, and countless relapses. It wasn't until she was court-ordered into a faith-based recovery program that she encountered worship.
The first time she heard live worship, something cracked inside her. *"I didn't know what that feeling was," she recalled. "I just started crying. I hadn't cried in years."*
The leaders encouraged her to attend worship night every evening. At first, she stood in the back, arms crossed. But night after night, she found herself stepping forward, then lifting her hands, then kneeling. One evening, during a spontaneous song that simply repeated *"You are worthy,"* she collapsed on the floor and began to scream—then sob—then laugh. Something left her.
Tamara was never the same. She began writing worship songs in her journal. She eventually completed her program, found a job at a local bakery, and now leads worship at her church's

recovery ministry. Her favorite Scripture? *Acts 16:25-26,* where Paul and Silas worshipped in prison and the chains literally fell off.

Worship did for Tamara what no human could—it bypassed her defenses and reached the part of her soul that still believed in freedom.

**From Panic to Praise: Anxiety and Depression**

Reuben Niles, a 22-year-old university student in Mumbai, battled severe panic attacks and suicidal thoughts. Though he had grown up in church, he viewed worship as a duty, not a lifeline. After one particularly dark night, he stumbled upon Psalm 42 and read aloud: *"Why, my soul, are you downcast?... Put your hope in God, for I will yet praise him."*

The phrase *"I will yet praise him"* haunted him. He began writing it on sticky notes and placing them around his room. He forced himself to play worship music the moment anxiety crept in. When the waves came, he sang—through the tears, through the trembling, even through gritted teeth.

One day, during a small worship gathering, someone prophetically sang *"God is breaking fear with His love."* Reuben collapsed to the floor and wept for almost an hour. The burden he had carried for four years was lifted.

Today, Reuben runs a blog called *Yet I Will Praise*, helping others navigate anxiety through worship and Scripture. Like King Jehoshaphat, who sent singers ahead of his army (2 Chronicles 20), Reuben learned that sometimes the only way through the battlefield of the mind is with a song.

**Worship on the Frontlines: Missionaries and Worship Leaders**

Marta and Julian Velasquez, missionaries in northern Colombia, served in a region plagued by guerrilla warfare and narcotics trafficking. Their home church in Bogotá had commissioned them not only to teach and disciple—but to *worship*. "Sing the sound of heaven over the land," their pastor had instructed.

At first, they thought it was symbolic. But after months of tension and threats, they started holding outdoor worship nights. Neighbors were hesitant. But slowly, curiosity brought them out. On one powerful night, as the team sang *"No Weapon Formed Against Me Shall Prosper"*, the local militia unexpectedly disbanded and surrendered their weapons. The next week, many of them came to the Velasquez home, asking to know more about this God of peace.

Years later, Marta reflected, "It wasn't our preaching that changed the region. It was the worship. It was heaven invading the noise of war."

Just as Joshua and the Israelites marched around Jericho with trumpets (Joshua 6), Marta and Julian learned that worship doesn't just transform hearts—it can disarm entire systems.

**City-Wide Awakening: Worship Movements that Transformed Culture**

In the heart of Wellington, New Zealand, a city-wide worship movement began with a 17-year-old named Isaac Murray. Troubled by rising youth violence and depression, he felt God instruct him during a morning devotion: *"Gather them to worship me."*

He had no platform, no funding—just faith. He contacted worship teams from local churches and booked a city park for a free worship night called

“One Sound”. Nearly 300 showed up. The next month—1,200. By the fifth gathering, over 5,000 people from all denominations and backgrounds were lifting their hands together in the cold New Zealand night.

Testimonies of healing, reconciliations, and spontaneous baptisms followed. Even the mayor attended, acknowledging the impact on public peace. Crime reports dipped, churches experienced revival, and high school prayer groups exploded across the city.

Much like the national repentance and revival under King Josiah (2 Kings 23), Wellington experienced a city-wide spiritual renewal—because one young man believed worship could change a culture.

**Closing Reflections**

These stories are not myths or exaggerated memoirs. They are the echoes of real journeys, fictionalized here to honor privacy but rooted in universal truth. Worship is not passive. It is not a filler between sermons. It is the sound of surrender, the scent of victory, and the language of heaven.

Each of these individuals—grieving, sick, addicted, anxious, and on the frontlines—found that breakthrough did not come when they tried harder, but when they worshipped deeper.

Their lives now sing what Psalm 126:1 declares: *“When the Lord restored the fortunes of Zion, we were like those who dreamed. Our mouths were filled with laughter, our tongues with songs of joy.”*

Worship will not only restore your heart.

It will rewrite your story.

# Chapter 16: Worship in the End Times – Preparing the Bride

The last days will not be marked merely by wars, famines, and lawlessness. They will be marked by worship—not confined to cathedrals or corners of the earth, but rising from every nation, tribe, and tongue. The prophets saw it. Jesus spoke of it. And the Spirit is stirring it now.

In Malachi 1:11, God declares: *"For from the rising of the sun even to its setting, My name will be great among the nations, and in every place incense is going to be offered to My name, and a grain offering that is pure; for My name will be great among the nations," says the Lord of hosts.*

This is not poetry. It is prophecy. It is the soundtrack of the end times.

In these final days, worship is not a side event in God's agenda. It is the preparation of the Bride, the declaration of war, and the intercession for the nations. This chapter journeys into that holy tension—between the now and the not yet—and reveals how worship is shaping eternity.

### The Rising Incense: A Prophetic Picture from India

Deepak and Anvi Rao, a humble couple in Udaipur, Rajasthan, had no global platform. Their church, tucked between stone houses, had fewer than 40 members. Yet every morning at sunrise, Deepak would rise to light incense and sing the names of

God in Hindi. His voice echoed through the narrow alleyways, waking neighbors and pigeons alike.

He wasn't trying to start a movement. He was simply fulfilling what he believed Malachi 1:11 commanded: *"From the rising of the sun..."* Deepak believed worship must rise before the world does.

One morning, a foreign missionary wandered into their home church. She wept during worship. Later, she told the Raos, *"When you sing, it smells like heaven here. I feel like I'm hearing the global Church wake up."*

What Deepak and Anvi didn't realize was that worship gatherings like theirs were springing up in Indonesia, Nigeria, Chile, and remote islands of the Philippines—small fires lit in obedience to the same scripture. In spiritual terms, a canopy of praise was forming across time zones.

The end times, they understood, would not be heralded by a shout from the elite but by the steady, daily rhythm of nameless worshippers offering "pure offerings" of praise.

Just as the wise men from the East brought incense to honor Jesus' first coming (Matthew 2:11), today's worshippers are offering it again—this time in preparation for His second.

**Worship as Bridal Preparation: The Story of Eleanor Briggs**

Eleanor Briggs, a 59-year-old widow from Yorkshire, England, lived alone in a countryside cottage. Her husband had passed ten years ago, and her children had moved far away. In the solitude, Eleanor cultivated what she called "Bridal Worship"—setting aside time each day to sit before God, light a candle, and sing songs of devotion as though preparing for a wedding.

It began after she read Revelation 19:7: *"Let us rejoice and be glad and give Him glory! For the wedding of the Lamb has come, and His bride has made herself ready."*

The verse ignited something deep in her. She realized the Church wasn't just waiting for Christ's return; she was meant to be preparing—adorning herself, purifying her love, learning His voice. Worship became Eleanor's way of brushing her gown, of waiting with oil in her lamp.

Her simple acts—prayers, songs, and Scripture recitations—carried an intensity that drew even her skeptical neighbors. Eventually, two teenage girls from her village began joining her once a week. They called it *Bride Night.* What began in a cottage became a weekly house gathering of nearly 20 young women, learning to worship like a Bride preparing for her Groom.

Eleanor often reminded them of the parable of the ten virgins in Matthew 25: *"Be ready, for the Bridegroom comes at an hour you do not expect." She would say, "We don't just wait. We worship while we wait."*

Worship in the end times is not about performance. It is about purity. It is not about talent. It is about longing. It is the language of the faithful waiting for the King.

**Intercession for Nations: Psalm 67 in the Mountains of Peru**

In the highlands of Peru, Luis Gutiérrez, a young Quechua believer, had a vision during a 3-day prayer fast. He saw a golden bowl being tipped over the

Andes mountains, and from it, rivers of light flowing toward every continent. He heard the Lord whisper: *"These are the prayers of worshipping nations."*

Luis had never traveled far from his village, but he had memorized Psalm 67, and especially clung to verse 3: *"Let the peoples praise you, O God; let all the peoples praise you."*

He began gathering small groups in the village square—not to protest or preach, but to worship in intercession. They would lift their hands and sing names of nations out loud: "Brazil, let the people praise Him! Turkey, let the people praise Him! China, let the people praise Him!"

At first, people laughed. But over time, a reverence settled over the gatherings. Teenagers began bringing flags. Older women started weaving nation names into blankets. What began as one man's obedience turned into a village-wide movement of intercessory worship for the nations.

Soon, news spread. Other villages followed. Regional pastors began teaching on Psalm 67, showing how praise for God among the nations leads to the earth yielding its harvest (Psalm 67:6). Luis and his community understood that worship wasn't just a response to revival—it was the road to it.

Like Anna the prophetess, who worshipped night and day in the temple awaiting redemption (Luke 2:36-38), Luis gave his life not to programs or fame—but to worship and watchfulness.

**The Song and the Shaking**

The end times will be marked by shakings—economic, political, moral. But as Hebrews 12:28 reminds us, *"Since we are receiving a kingdom that cannot be shaken, let us be thankful, and so worship God acceptably with reverence and awe."*

We are not called to fear the shaking.

We are called to sing through it.

Worship is how the Bride steadies herself. It is how she stays pure in a polluted world. It is how she lifts her voice above the noise, keeping her eyes on the Bridegroom instead of the storm.

The global rise in worship is not coincidence—it is a divine summons. From underground churches in Iran to megachurches in Seoul, from tribal chants in Kenya to harp and bowl sessions in Kansas City, worship is uniting heaven and earth, and accelerating the return of the King.

Jesus told the Samaritan woman, *"A time is coming and has now come when the true worshipers will worship the Father in spirit and truth."* (John 4:23). That time is now.

**Closing Reflections**

The Church in the end times will not be known for her strategy or her systems. She will be known by her song—a song that spans nations, races, generations, and languages.

Worship is not just the atmosphere of heaven.

It is the invitation to live ready.

The Bride is not just waiting. She is singing. She is adorning herself with praise, purity, and purpose. She is interceding for nations, watching for the clouds, lighting her lamps.

And when the trumpet sounds, it will not be a surprise to her.

She will already be singing.

# Chapter 17: Raising a Worship Generation

In an age where screens flicker brighter than candles and attention spans are scattered across notifications and noise, the holy art of worship can be easily lost between generations. Yet God's design has never changed. Worship was never meant to remain in the sanctuary. It was always meant to begin at the dining table, continue on evening walks, and echo in the bedrooms of children being tucked in at night.

The Lord said through Moses:

*"Hear, O Israel: The Lord our God, the Lord is one. Love the Lord your God with all your heart and with all your soul and with all your strength. These commandments that I give you today are to be on your hearts. Impress them on your children. Talk about them when you sit at home and when you walk along the road, when you lie down and when you get up." (Deuteronomy 6:4–7)*

This is the heartbeat of generational worship. Impress them. Talk about them. Live them. Worship must be seen, heard, and inherited—not just sung.

**Teaching Worship to Children and Youth: The Story of the Abebayo Family**

In Lagos, Nigeria, Pastor Tobi Abebayo and his wife Remi had three children between the ages of 8 and 16. The Abebayo home was filled with life—football gear by the front door, half-finished art projects on the dining table, and the smell of Remi's spicy jollof rice in the air.

Tobi, a worship pastor, had a firm belief: "My children won't learn worship because I sing on stage. They'll learn it when I teach them to kneel beside me in our living room."

So every Saturday night, the Abebayos gathered in their modest sitting room for what they called "The Family Altar." Tobi would lead a short time of worship on his acoustic guitar. Sometimes it was a full session; other times, just one heartfelt song followed by prayer. There were nights of laughter when their youngest, Zina, sang off-key, and nights of tears when their oldest, Joshua, shared struggles from school.

But more than the songs, it was the intentional space that mattered.

Remi began teaching her children what each song meant. When they sang *"You are Yahweh"*, she explained the covenant name of God from Exodus 3:14. When they sang *"Way Maker"*, she told the story of the Red Sea parting in Exodus 14. Songs were not just melodies; they became living theology for their children.

One night, during a school worship event, their daughter Zara, just 10, raised her hands and began spontaneously singing a Scripture from Psalm 23 in front of her classmates. Her teacher, a new believer, was moved to tears. Later, she confessed that Zara's worship led her to open her Bible for the first time in years.

Worship isn't taught in lectures. It's caught in the atmosphere of reverence. And that atmosphere starts in homes like the Abebayo's—where children learn that worship is not performance, but relationship.

**Family Worship Practices: The Ellsworths of Vermont**

Miles and Eliza Ellsworth, a couple in rural Vermont, were far from charismatic by personality. Miles was an introverted book editor, and Eliza, a midwife with long shifts and unpredictable hours. But what they lacked in outward expression, they made up for in quiet, consistent devotion.

Each morning before sunrise, Miles would light a candle on the breakfast table and read aloud a short Psalm while the coffee brewed. Their daughters, Lucy (13) and Nora (9), would sit sleepily beside him, heads on folded arms. Eliza, if home, would join them, humming softly.

This routine wasn't glamorous. There were no instruments, no loud declarations, no ecstatic encounters. But there was presence. And that presence was shaping a legacy of stillness and intimacy with God.

The Ellsworths clung to Psalm 46:10—*"Be still and know that I am God."* Their home became a place where silence was sacred and singing was a whispered offering, especially before meals and bedtime.

Years later, when Lucy went off to college, she called her father one morning and said, "Dad, I woke up early and read Psalm 91. I lit a candle. I could almost smell your coffee. I think... worship lives in me now."

Family worship doesn't always look like a choir. Sometimes it looks like gentle repetition, quiet reverence, and a family choosing to make God visible in ordinary mornings.

Just as Noah built an altar for his family after the flood (Genesis 8:20), Miles and Eliza were building one in Vermont—brick by brick, verse by verse, morning by morning.

## Generational Legacy: The Life of Bishop Elias Navarro

In the outskirts of Bogotá, Colombia, Bishop Elias Navarro stood at 76 years of age, leading a thriving congregation of over 3,000. But what stirred his heart most wasn't the size of his church—it was the sound of his 17-year-old granddaughter, Catalina, leading worship on Sunday mornings.

Elias often recounted to his congregation how his mother, Maria Navarro, had once worshiped alone in the fields while working as a coffee picker in the 1940s. With a child strapped to her back, she would sing hymns and Scripture out loud for the mountains to hear.

"She planted songs in soil," Elias would say. "And now those songs have grown into trees bearing fruit for generations."

Maria taught her son the Shema (Deuteronomy 6:4–9) and insisted that every Scripture memorized was a stone laid on the altar of their future. Elias, in turn, did the same with his children, and now Catalina was carrying that altar into a new generation.

When asked by a reporter how his church had sustained revival for over 40 years, Bishop Elias simply said, "We sing the same songs our abuelas sang in the fields. We don't forget who taught us to sing."

This is the true generational legacy of worship. Not flashy trends or new compositions, but the handing down of a song, like passing a torch in a long relay.

The psalmist wrote in Psalm 145:4: *"One generation shall commend your works to another, and shall declare your mighty acts."*
Elias Navarro embodied this. His mother worshipped in the fields. He worshipped in pulpits. His granddaughter worshipped through livestreams and digital spaces. Three generations. One God. One song echoing through time.

**The Enduring Impact of Family Worship**
In every corner of the world—rural and urban, rich and poor, expressive and contemplative—families are shaping future worshippers not by chance, but by choice.
Just as Timothy learned the Scriptures from his grandmother Lois and mother Eunice (2 Timothy 1:5), today's children are learning how to worship by watching what we value.
*When parents worship through tears…*
*When mothers sing through sleepless nights…*
*When fathers open the Word before breakfast…*
*When siblings pray for each other…*
*Worship becomes more than an activity.*
*It becomes inheritance*.
The task of raising a worship generation does not rest on pastors alone. It rests in homes, dinner tables, night-time routines, and the deliberate decision to live lives that make God glorious, not only in church, but in everyday moments.

**Building a Family Altar That Lasts**
The altar is not made of stone anymore. It's built of time, truth, and togetherness.
It's built when parents make room in the schedule to pray as a family.

It's built when Scripture is not only quoted but lived.
It's built when worship is not an obligation but a delight passed down.
The greatest worship movement will not come from a stage.
It will come from living rooms, bedrooms, and kitchen tables—where one generation worships in front of the next.
Let us rise, then, as worshipping families.
Let us raise a generation who doesn't just sing songs—but sings them with revelation, reverence, and relationship.
Because what we build today… they will carry tomorrow.

# Conclusion: Our Eternal Identity – Worshippers Forever

The final curtain of history will not fall in silence. It will rise to the thunderous sound of worship—voices from every tribe, every language, every generation lifted as one in adoration of the Lamb. There, at the center of all time and eternity, worship will not end. It will begin anew.

The apostle John, exiled and alone on the island of Patmos, was granted a window into this eternal reality. His words shimmer with awe:

"After this I looked, and there before me was a great multitude that no one could count, from every nation, tribe, people and language, standing before the throne and before the Lamb. They were wearing white robes and were holding palm branches in their hands. And they cried out in a loud voice: 'Salvation belongs to our God, who sits on the throne, and to the Lamb.'" *(Revelation 7:9–10)*

This is our destiny—not merely to believe, or to serve, or to endure, but to worship forever. Worship is not simply an earthly discipline. It is our eternal identity.

**From Earth to Eternity: The Journey of Worship**

For Adelaide Mofokeng, an elderly widow in Soweto, South Africa, worship had always been a lifeline. In her small home filled with the scent of rooibos tea and hand-sewn tapestries, she would sit each morning with a worn Bible and sing softly to the Lord. Her voice, though aged, held a youthful joy. She had buried her husband in apartheid times, lost two sons to gang violence, and faced years of loneliness. But she would say, "When I sing, I remember I'm not alone. Heaven listens."

Adelaide died peacefully in her sleep at age 91. Her granddaughter, Naledi, said later, "I heard her whispering a song in her last breath—*'Worthy is the Lamb.'* That's how she entered eternity... worshipping."

Her journey—marked by sorrow, perseverance, and song—is not unique. Every believer walks this road. We worship in the valleys, we sing through the shadows, and at the end, we do not fall into silence—we rise into glory.

In the words of the psalmist:

"I will sing to the Lord all my life; I will sing praise to my God as long as I live." *(Psalm 104:33)*

But there comes a moment when "as long as I live" becomes forever. Worship does not stop when breath ceases—it expands, liberated from the confines of earthly pain, perfected in the presence of the Lamb.

**The Eternal Assembly: A Tapestry of Worship**

In *Revelation 7:9–12*, we behold a choir that is unlike any the earth has ever seen.

Not a single voice, but a multitude.

Not a solo, but a symphony.

Not one tongue, but thousands—Zarma, Farsi, Quechua, Tagalog, Swahili—all declaring one truth: "Salvation belongs to our God!"

Imagine the sound.

Imagine the moment.

Every martyr and missionary. Every child taught to worship in a family home. Every elderly saint who

sang alone at dawn. Every imprisoned believer who whispered praises through tears.
They are all there. Together. Loud. Free. Eternal.
Among them might be Nicolas Duval, a quiet Parisian violinist who once battled suicidal depression. He found Jesus through music therapy at a Christian rehabilitation center. The song *"How Deep the Father's Love for Us"* became his anchor. He would later lead worship in a small underground church for recovering addicts. Today, he rests in glory, his instrument traded for a crown—but he still plays, still sings.
Or Hana Takamoto, a schoolteacher in Tokyo who came to Christ through an online Bible study. She worshiped in secret, hiding her faith from her hostile family. Her only sanctuary was her classroom after hours, where she played instrumental worship songs on the piano in the dark, the Spirit of God her only audience. Hana's story will be known on that day—not for earthly fame, but for eternal faithfulness.
These are the worshippers forever. They are you and me.
This multitude is not a fantasy—it is a future guaranteed by the blood of the Lamb.

**Final Charge: Arise, Worshipping Warrior!**
As this book closes, let the final word be not just a reflection—but a summons.
***You were made to worship.***
*Before you were a worker, a parent, a leader, a thinker—you were created to adore.*
*Before you were called to serve, you were called to behold.*
*Before battles were fought, songs were written.*

*Before there was a throne to rule on earth, there was a throne to bow before in heaven.*
*Worship is not weakness. It is warfare.*
*It is not an escape. It is an entrance into the authority of heaven.*
*It is not an emotion. It is a weapon.*
***Arise, Worshipping Warrior!***
Let your voice be heard in this age—so that it echoes in the age to come.
Worship in your home.
Worship in your school.
Worship in your office.
Worship when it's raining.
Worship when it hurts.
Worship when it costs.
Worship until the King returns.
For when the Son of Man descends in glory, He is not returning for entertainers, nor theologians, nor strategists.
He is returning for a Bride who worships.
Let your life be that fragrant offering, poured at His feet.
Let your legacy be that of one who never stopped singing—even in the silence.
Let your story end the way it will begin again in eternity:
Face down, palms raised, eyes fixed… Crying with all the saints and angels:
*"Amen! Praise and glory and wisdom and thanks and honor and power and strength be to our God forever and ever. Amen!" (Revelation 7:12)*

# Appendix A: Top 50 Scriptures on Worship and Warfare

1. 2 Chronicles 20:22 – *As they began to sing and praise, the Lord set ambushes against their enemies.*
2. Psalm 149:6–9 – *Let the high praises of God be in their mouths and a double-edged sword in their hands.*
3. Ephesians 6:12 – *For our struggle is not against flesh and blood...*
4. Psalm 144:1 – *Praise be to the Lord my Rock, who trains my hands for war.*
5. Acts 16:25–26 – *Paul and Silas prayed and sang hymns... and the prison doors flew open.*
6. Isaiah 30:32 – *Every stroke the Lord lays on them with His punishing club will be to the music of tambourines and harps.*
7. Hebrews 13:15 – *Let us continually offer to God a sacrifice of praise.*
8. Exodus 15:2–3 – *The Lord is my strength and my defense... The Lord is a warrior.*
9. Psalm 18:3 – *I called to the Lord, who is worthy of praise, and I have been saved from my enemies.*
10. 2 Corinthians 10:4 – *The weapons we fight with are not the weapons of the world...*
11. Revelation 19:11–16 – *The Rider on the white horse... His name is The Word of God.*
12. Psalm 22:3 – *God inhabits the praises of His people.*

13. Joshua 6:20 – *When the people shouted, the wall collapsed...*
14. Isaiah 42:10–13 – *Sing to the Lord a new song... The Lord will march out like a champion.*
15. Zephaniah 3:17 – *He rejoices over you with singing.*
16. Psalm 68:1 – *Let God arise, let His enemies be scattered.*
17. 1 Samuel 16:23 – *David played his harp and the evil spirit left Saul.*
18. Psalm 98:1 – *Sing to the Lord a new song, for He has done marvelous things.*
19. Revelation 5:8–10 – *The elders fell down before the Lamb with harps and golden bowls of incense.*
20. Psalm 91:1–4 – *He who dwells in the secret place of the Most High shall abide under the shadow of the Almighty.*
21. Isaiah 61:3 – *A garment of praise instead of a spirit of despair.*
22. 1 Chronicles 16:23–25 – *Sing to the Lord, all the earth... For great is the Lord.*
23. 2 Kings 3:15 – *When the musician played, the hand of the Lord came upon him.*
24. Psalm 33:3 – *Sing to Him a new song; play skillfully, and shout for joy.*
25. Romans 12:1–2 – *Offer your bodies as a living sacrifice, holy and pleasing to God—this is your true and proper worship.*
26. Isaiah 6:1–4 – *The whole earth is full of His glory... the thresholds shook at the sound of their voices.*
27. Psalm 95:1–3 – *Let us sing for joy to the Lord... For the Lord is the great God.*

28. Revelation 7:9–12 – *A great multitude... cried out in a loud voice: "Salvation belongs to our God!"*
29. Judges 7:20–22 – *The 300 blew their trumpets... and the enemy turned on each other.*
30. Habakkuk 3:17–19 – *Yet I will rejoice in the Lord; I will be joyful in God my Savior.*
31. Psalm 42:11 – *Put your hope in God, for I will yet praise Him.*
32. John 4:23–24 – *True worshipers will worship the Father in the Spirit and in truth.*
33. Philippians 4:6–7 – *With thanksgiving, present your requests to God... and the peace of God will guard your hearts.*
34. Romans 8:37–39 – *In all these things we are more than conquerors through Him who loved us.*
35. Psalm 34:1 – *I will bless the Lord at all times; His praise shall continually be in my mouth.*
36. 2 Chronicles 5:13–14 – *The trumpeters and musicians joined in unison... the glory of the Lord filled the temple.*
37. Nehemiah 8:10 – *The joy of the Lord is your strength.*
38. 1 Peter 2:9 – *You are a chosen people... that you may declare the praises of Him.*
39. Revelation 14:2–3 – *A sound like harpists playing their harps... they sang a new song before the throne.*
40. Psalm 9:1–3 – *I will praise You, Lord, with all my heart... My enemies turn back and perish before You.*
41. Isaiah 12:5 – *Sing to the Lord, for He has done glorious things.*

42. Psalm 100:4 – *Enter His gates with thanksgiving and His courts with praise.*
43. Deuteronomy 20:4 – *For the Lord your God is the One who goes with you to fight for you.*
44. Colossians 3:16–17 – *Sing psalms, hymns, and spiritual songs with gratitude in your hearts to God.*
45. Psalm 3:3 – *But You, Lord, are a shield around me, my glory, the One who lifts my head high.*
46. Matthew 21:16 – *From the lips of children and infants You have ordained praise.*
47. Psalm 108:1–3 – *I will sing and make music with all my soul.*
48. Joel 3:9–10 – *Proclaim this among the nations: Prepare for war!*
49. Psalm 27:6 – *I will offer sacrifices with shouts of joy; I will sing and make music to the Lord.*
50. 1 Thessalonians 5:16–18 – *Rejoice always, pray continually, give thanks in all circumstances.*

# Appendix B:
# 31 Daily Worship Declarations

**Living Victoriously Through the Power of Praise**
These daily declarations are meant to be spoken aloud in faith each morning or night, activating worship as a weapon of spiritual warfare, breakthrough, and victory. Each one is anchored in truth and rooted in the reality of God's supremacy and the power of worship.

---

Day 1:
*Today, I lift up my voice in praise and scatter the plans of the enemy. My worship summons the presence of God and shifts the battle in my favor.*
Day 2:
*When I worship, heaven moves on my behalf. My praise is not passive—it is a weapon of war and a shield of faith.*
Day 3:
*Every melody I sing in worship becomes a sword in the Spirit, striking down fear, anxiety, and doubt.*
Day 4:
*My worship breaks chains in the unseen realm. As Paul and Silas sang, so I sing—and doors are opening and shackles are falling.*
Day 5:
*I declare that worship invites divine strategy. As Jehoshaphat sent out singers, I go before my battles with songs of victory.*
Day 6:
*Today, I sing not because everything is perfect, but because my God is. My worship confuses the enemy's camp.*

Day 7:
*In my praise, the Lord fights for me. I stand still and see the salvation of my God as I worship in faith.*
Day 8:
*Worship lifts me above the noise of the world and tunes my heart to the voice of the Commander of Heaven's Armies.*
Day 9:
*I declare that the presence of God, drawn through worship, disarms every attack and silences every lie.*
Day 10:
*The more I worship, the less room I give to worry. I exchange ashes for beauty and heaviness for the garment of praise.*
Day 11:
*I shout with joy before the battle is over. My praise is prophetic—it speaks victory before I see it.*
Day 12:
*My praise builds a throne for God in my circumstances. He is enthroned in my worship, and where He reigns, darkness flees.*
Day 13:
*I will not be silent. My song is warfare, my declaration is defiance, and my worship is a war cry against the enemy.*
Day 14:
*As I worship, angels are dispatched, strongholds are demolished, and divine order is released.*
Day 15:
*My heart is a battlefield, but worship is my peacekeeper. I win wars in my soul by magnifying the One who never loses.*
Day 16:
*I declare that worship is my protest against evil and*

*injustice. I exalt the King of kings above all earthly rulers.*

Day 17:

*Worship realigns my perspective—I see victory, not defeat. I see the Cross, not the chaos.*

Day 18:

*As I lift my voice in worship today, confusion enters the enemy's camp. God is arising, and His enemies are scattering before my praise.*

Day 19:

*Worship is my spiritual roar—it terrifies the enemy and testifies of my trust in the One who cannot be defeated.*

Day 20:

*When I sing, I silence the accuser. Worship cancels the lies of the enemy and establishes truth in my atmosphere.*

Day 21:

*My praise today is a prophetic strike against every stronghold. I release worship to tear down walls like Jericho's.*

Day 22:

*I declare that worship opens heavenly portals. As I praise, divine resources, revelations, and reinforcements are released.*

Day 23:

*I wield worship like a warrior's sword. My melodies are not weak—they are powerful and mighty through God to demolish strongholds.*

Day 24:

*Today, I clothe myself with the garment of praise and strip off the spirit of heaviness. My worship is my warfare wardrobe.*

Day 25:

*Every word of worship I speak becomes a*

*declaration of God's dominion and a blow to the kingdom of darkness.*

Day 26:

*In worship, I rise above my battles. I ascend into the throne room, where victory is already secured.*

Day 27:

*As I worship, my spiritual enemies are exposed and expelled. Praise illuminates the battlefield and brings clarity and courage.*

Day 28:

*I sing ahead of the miracle. My worship makes way for divine intervention even before I see it with my eyes.*

Day 29:

*Worship is my strategy against weariness. I don't give up—I lift up! And as I lift up praise, strength returns to my soul.*

Day 30:

*I declare that worship rebukes the devourer. The sound of praise shuts the mouth of the lion and quenches the fire of the furnace.*

Day 31:

*Today, I take territory through worship. I am not retreating—I'm advancing. My praise is my banner, my breakthrough, and my battle cry!*

# Appendix C:
# Family Worship Guide

*Helping Families Worship Together in Spirit and in Truth*

**Purpose:**

This guide provides a weekly family worship rhythm, combining Scripture, music, prayer, and discussion. It's designed to foster a lifestyle of worship in the home—where children and adults alike learn to use praise as a powerful weapon in everyday life.

---

**Weekly Structure:**

**Day 1: Set the Atmosphere – Building the Altar at Home**

- ✓ Read: Joshua 24:15 – "As for me and my house, we will serve the Lord."
- ✓ Activity: Let each family member light a candle or place a symbolic stone to represent building an altar at home.
- ✓ Worship Song: "Here I Am to Worship" or any simple, heartfelt worship song.
- ✓ Prayer: Invite God's presence into your home and rededicate your family to Him.

**Day 2: Worship as Thanksgiving**

- ✓ Read: Psalm 100
- ✓ Activity: Each person shares one thing they are thankful for.
- ✓ Worship Song: "Give Thanks"
- ✓ Reflection: How does gratitude shift your heart and mind?

**Day 3: Worship as Warfare**

- ✓ Read: 2 Chronicles 20:21–22

- ✓ Activity: March around your home declaring God's promises out loud.
- ✓ Worship Song: "Surrounded (Fight My Battles)"
- ✓ Family Discussion: What battles are we facing as a family? How can we respond in worship?

**Day 4: Worship in Hard Times**

- ✓ Read: Acts 16:25–26
- ✓ Activity: Act out Paul and Silas worshiping in prison.
- ✓ Worship Song: "Raise a Hallelujah"
- ✓ Prayer: Ask God to release breakthrough for anyone feeling bound or discouraged.

**Day 5: Generational Worship**

- ✓ Read: Deuteronomy 6:4–9
- ✓ Activity: Create a "family worship journal" to pass down experiences and prayers.
- ✓ Worship Song: "The Blessing"
- ✓ Declaration: Speak God's promises over the next generation.

**Day 6: Prophetic Worship**

- ✓ Read: Isaiah 61:3
- ✓ Activity: Ask each person to write or draw what God is saying to them in worship.
- ✓ Worship Song: "Way Maker"
- ✓ Discussion: How can our worship shift the spiritual climate?

**Day 7: Celebration Worship**

- ✓ Read: Psalm 150
- ✓ Activity: Use instruments (real or handmade) and have a joyful worship session.
- ✓ Worship Song: Any joyful praise song.
- ✓ Family Reflection: What has God done for us this week?

# Appendix D: Small Group / Church Study Questions by Chapter

*Going Deeper in Community and Application*

Each chapter contains reflection and discussion questions suitable for small groups, worship teams, or congregational study.

---

**Chapter 1: The Heart of Worship**

- ✓ What does it mean to worship "in spirit and in truth" in your daily life?
- ✓ How do we distinguish between performance and true worship?

**Chapter 2: Worship as Identity**

- ✓ How does being created to worship impact how you see yourself?
- ✓ In what ways can we protect and cultivate our identity as worshipers?

**Chapter 3: From the Valley to the Throne**

- ✓ Share a time when worship helped you in a low season.
- ✓ What spiritual discipline do you practice when you don't "feel" like worshiping?

**Chapter 4: Worship in the Wilderness**

- ✓ How did Jesus use worship and the Word during His wilderness temptation?
- ✓ What can we learn from Israel's worship (and lack thereof) in the desert?

**Chapter 5: The Sound of Deliverance**

- ✓ What role does sound play in spiritual breakthrough?
- ✓ Do you use music and singing in your personal prayer time? Why or why not?

**Chapter 6: Worship in the Midnight Hour**

- ✓ Why is worship especially powerful during dark times?
- ✓ Who in Scripture inspires you most in worship under pressure?

**Chapter 7: David's Tabernacle and Today's Worshiper**

- ✓ What set David's worship apart from others?
- ✓ How can we create a lifestyle of "tabernacle worship" today?

**Chapter 8: The Priesthood of All Believers**

- ✓ What does it mean that you are a "royal priest"?
- ✓ How can you lead your family or community in worship more intentionally?

**Chapter 9: The Tabernacle Pattern for Intimacy**

- ✓ Which part of the tabernacle do you identify with most in this season?
- ✓ How does the pattern of the tabernacle help you draw closer to God?

**Chapter 10: The Power of His Presence**

- ✓ How does practicing God's presence change the way you worship?
- ✓ Have you ever experienced His tangible presence in worship?

**Chapter 11: Strategic Worship for the Battle**

- ✓ How can we use worship both offensively and defensively in spiritual battles?
- ✓ Share a personal or biblical example of worship turning the tide of warfare.

**Chapter 12: Prophetic & Apostolic Worship**

- ✓ What does it mean to sing the Word or declare God's names prophetically?
- ✓ How does apostolic worship differ from traditional expressions?

**Chapter 13: Worship That Breaks Strongholds**

- ✓ How have you seen worship help someone overcome addiction, fear, or sin?
- ✓ What generational chains need breaking in your family line through worship?

**Chapter 14: 30-Day Practical Action Plan**

- ✓ Which week of the action plan do you find most challenging and why?
- ✓ How can we hold each other accountable to live a lifestyle of worship?

**Chapter 15: Breakthrough Through Worship**

- ✓ Which testimony stood out to you most and why?
- ✓ What is your own worship testimony—how has God met you in praise?

**Chapter 16: Worship in the End Times – Preparing the Bride**

- ✓ What does Malachi 1:11 mean in your context?

- ✓ How can worship prepare both individuals and the church for Christ's return?

**Chapter 17: Raising a Worship Generation**

- ✓ How can we make worship part of our family rhythm?
- ✓ What legacy are you leaving through your worship?

**Conclusion: Our Eternal Identity – Worshippers Forever**

- ✓ How does the vision in Revelation 7:9–12 inspire your worship now?
- ✓ What does it mean to arise as a worshiping warrior in this generation?

---

# About the Author 'GERARD ASSEY'

Gerard Assey is a Graduate in Economics, a PGD in Management (HRD) and holds a Doctorate in Leadership. Gerard holds several International Qualifications in Sales, Debt Collection, Training & Teaching, and is a 'Fellow' of the prestigious 'Institute of Sales & Marketing Management'-UK, a Certified NLP Practitioner, a 'Certified Trainer', an 'Accredited Management Teacher-Behavioral Sciences', a 'Certified Competency Facilitator', a 'Certified Management Consultant'- (the International credentials of a professional management consultant, awarded in accordance with global standards of the ICMCI); and a Certification from the University of Michigan in 'Successful Negotiation: Essential Strategies and Skills'

He is also a Member of the 'National Association of Sales Professionals' backed with several years experience in varied industries, both in India and Overseas. He also holds an 'Etiquette Consultant' Certification from the USA (by Sue Fox, Author of Best Seller: 'Business Etiquette for Dummies'. She has trained some of the top celebrities' world over). He was also a recipient of a scholarship for extensive training in Japan on 'Corporate Management for India'.

Gerard Assey is 'Founder & Chief Corporate Trainer' of the Group: '**Citius, Altius, Fortius Unlimited**'- an organization that **celebrated 20 years of Glorious Service** in 2021, focusing on 3 Core Competencies:

**People. Performance. Profit**; in functional areas of Sales & Marketing, HR & Organizational Development, covering Recruitment, Training & Consultancy!
Having managed organizations with large Sales Forces in India & Overseas, his specialization cover extensive areas of Sales Training (All levels - Presentation, Negotiation, Key/ Strategic Accounts Management & Managerial Skills for all sectors), Bid Proposal/ Capture Planning/ Management Trainings, Retail Sales, Customer Service & Customer Retention Programs, Training for Prevention & Collection of Debt, Self & Personal Development Programs (Time Management, Teamwork & Team Building, Business Etiquette & Personal Grooming, Leadership & Managerial Skills, People Management Skills, Train-the-Trainer etc), including preparation of Custom-designed Business Manuals for Internal (HR, Induction, and Sales etc) & External use (Instruction, User Manuals).
Gerard has successfully conducted over 6450 Trainings & Workshops (as of April '25) all across India, Middle East, Africa, Europe & S.E. Asia. Besides public programs conducted regularly, both in India & Overseas, he has some of the top names as clients whom he services from Single Owners to large Public & Government undertakings, covering all sectors, for their in-house needs.
His website: www.CollectionSkills.com is the only one in this part of the world to be featured in the 'Collections & Credit Risk Magazine-USA' under 'Who's Who in Training' and ranks TOP, along with other websites listed below on most search engines.

**Gerard is author of 190 books already (May 2025)**, all the books being available on all online platforms and outlets as E-books and Paperbacks

**A few of our business related books:**

1. Bite-sized Bits on Commonsense Management
2. Heart to Heart on Life's Principles'
3. How to become a Successful Manager
4. The Sales Professionals' Master Workbook of S.Y.S.T.E.M.S
5. The Professional Business Email Etiquette Handbook & Guide
6. The Professional Business Video-Conferencing Etiquette Handbook & Guide
7. Professional Presentation Skills
8. Exceptional Customer Service
9. Professional Tele-Marketing Skills
10. Professional Debt Collection Skills
11. The G.R.E.A.T. Sales & Service Workbook
12. Sales Training Advantage for Results (*The Ultimate Sales Training Manual to enable you stand out as a S.T.A.R.*)
13. CEO Daily Planner & Organizer
14. The Sales Professionals' Master Daily Planner
15. The Professional Debt Collector's Master Daily Planner
16. My Daily Planner & Organizer
17. MY EMERGENCY INFORMATION RECORD (Family Emergency & Peace of Mind Planner)
18. The Ultimate Therapist & Counselors Planner and Organizer
19. Building an Ethical Workplace
20. Managing Relationships at Work
21. Managing Business Meetings Effectively
22. Effective Delegation Skills
23. Goal Setting for Success
24. B2B Selling by Email
25. Professional Business Etiquette & Grooming
26. Dining Etiquette & Table Manners
27. Effective Networking Skills
28. Grooming, Etiquette & Manners for Teens, Young Adults & Future Leaders
29. Inter-Personal Skills
30. Get Ready, Get Hired!
31. Selling in a Recession
32. Effective Receivables Management in an Economic Downturn!
33. Real Estate & Property Sales Training
34. Credit Sales & Accounts Receivable Management

35. Selling Skills for Real Estate & Property Advisors
36. Take G.R.E.A.T. C.A.R.E!
37. Spa, Salon & Health Club Selling Skills
38. Selling Travel, Holiday & MICE Services
39. Selling Skills for Spa's, Salons & Health Clubs
40. Retailing in Salons & Spas
41. Selling Holiday, Vacation, Tours & Packages
42. The Power of Sales Referrals
43. Selling Luxury
44. Technical Selling Skills
45. Financial Advisors Sales Training
46. Dealing with Burnout at Work Monopolize Your Markets
47. Selling to Affluent Customers
48. Growing up with Grace
49. Financial Selling Skills
50. *The Effective Manager's Guide: Key Skills to Thrive*
51. From Aspiring to Inspiring: A Guide for New Managers on the Rise
52. The Power of Focus
53. Selling with Integrity: Sell Like Jesus The Perfect Role Model!
54. 31 Habits of Champions: Your 31-Day Journey to Greatness
55. Rejecting Grasshopper Talk: From Grasshopper to Giant-Killer-*Defeating Giants Daily!*
56. Navigate the AI-Powered Future of Bid & Proposals: Up-Skill to Stay Relevant with Alternative Career Paths & Opportunities
57. Hiring Sales Winners
58. Present with Impact
59. Success Unlocked: *Breaking Free from Habits that Hold You Back*
60. Complaints to Cheers, Feedback to Gold: Mastering Complaints Management
61. Thriving Together: *Cultivating Diversity, Equity, and Inclusion*
62. Coaching Skills for Sales Managers
63. Soaring to Success in Business & Leadership: Swifter, Higher, Stronger!
64. From Classroom to Podium: A Student's Guide to Powerful Public Speaking & Presentation Skills
65. Developing Self-Discipline
66. The CEO's 31-Day Power Plan: Unlocking Success through Essential Traits

67. Credibility Matters
68. A Winning Attitude
69. Bid & Proposal Management Using AI
70. Sales Forecasting: A Practical & Proven Guide to Strategic Sales Forecasting
71. Elevate & Energize: *50 Dynamic & Fun Activities for Peak Workplace Morale*
72. 'Sales SOS! Sales on Fire! *30 Days to Conquer Chaos & the Nightmares of Success!'*
73. Mastering Sales Managerial Skills: *Building High-Performing Teams & Driving Exceptional Results*
74. Eagle-Eyed Leadership: Unleashing the Power of 31 Lessons from Eagles
75. The Ultimate Employee Training Guide: *Training Today, Leading Tomorrow*
76. Being More Accountable at Work
77. Creating a Culture of Continuous Improvement
78. Effective Questioning & Listening Skills
79. The Power of Value Selling
80. The Growth Mindset
81. Mastering Professional Help Desk Skills
82. The Power to Lead with Empathy
83. Being Prepared: The Key to Unlocking Success
84. Youthful Spark-Youth Energizers, Activities and Games-Igniting the Fun in Youth
85. Ignite your Motivation for Success
86. Elevate Your Executive Presence: *Your Roadmap to Executive Excellence*
87. Smart Decisions: *Mastering Problem Solving with Strategic Solutions for Business Success*
88. Strategic Planning: *Developing and Implementing Strategic Plans to Achieve Long-Term Business Goals*
89. The Power of Stay Interviews
90. Developing G.R.I.T.
91. Adaptability
92. Diagnosis- *A Key Skill for Leadership*
93. The Burnout-Proof Salesperson: *The Master Guide to Preventing Stress & Burnout-* Strategies for Thriving in Sales
94. Learning from Failure: *Keys to Success*
95. Customer Success Management
96. Overcoming the Killers of Motivation
97. The C-Suite Code: *Mastering Skills for Executive Excellence'*

98. Dealing with Difficult Customers
99. Unlocking Your Potential: Mastering the Top 20 Life Skills for a Brighter Future
100. Nurturing Tomorrow's Leaders: *Essential Soft Skills Every Child Must Learn*
101. Lively & Fun Party Games for Seniors & Elders
102. Role Playing for Sales Champions: From Practice to Performance
103. Fun and Exciting Party Games for Kids
104. Case Studies for Sales
105. Role-Playing for Unbeatable Customer Service
106. Case Studies in Customer Service
107. Case Studies in Winning Negotiations
108. Case Studies in Management & Leadership
109. Case Studies in Human Resources & Talent Management
110. CEO Success Blueprint: The Essential Toolkit for CEOs and C-Level Executives
111. The Salesperson's Self-Coaching Guide: *Master Your Own Self-Coaching Plan for Success*
112. Overcoming Procrastination: *Your Ultimate Guide to Stop Delaying and Start Living Your Best Life*
113. When True Colors Are Exposed: *The Journey to Unmasking Humanity*
114. Life-Changing Habits for Teens: Teen Success Blueprint for a Bright Future
115. Workplace Stress-Free: *Proven Strategies to Thrive at Work and Beyond*
116. Objection Overruled: *The Ultimate Guide to Turning 'No' into 'Yes'*
117. Building Strong Teams: *A Comprehensive Guide to Team Building*
118. Ethical & Moral Leadership in Business: *Eliminating Unethical Practices & Building a Culture of Trust & Integrity*

From the Ministry side, Gerard graduated in the very first batch of Charis Bible College-India & had for over 9 years served as a Part-time Faculty at Charis Bible College-Chennai (Andrew Wommack Ministries-Colorado, USA). He also holds a Diploma in Worship (a subject closest to his heart) from the JSOW and is also a graduate of the Advanced Mentorship Program (AMP) and the Circle Of

Ministerial Engagement (C.O.M.E.) of Prophet Jerome Fernando and a Spiritual Son of the Esteemed Prophet.
An accomplished author of several Secular & Christian Books, Gerard has been on the board of a few international organizations and boasts of being the SON of the MOST HIGH GOD: An ordinary guy following an extraordinary GOD!

**...And some of his most recent Christian Books being:**

1. A Bouquet of Praises for My KING
2. Christian Jokes for the Serious Religious' Folks!
3. Jesus Healed You!
4. Praise24Ever! (also in Tamil version)
5. The 5G Network of GOD
6. Building Faith over F.E.A.R- FACE EVERYTHING AND RISE with JESUS
7. Hebrew and Greek Praise and Worship Words
8. Godly Mothers' and Grandmothers' Bible Story time for Kids!
9. Miracles of Jesus in Pictures
10. Raise your Praise all 365 Days
11. Thanking GOD with an Attitude of Gratitude
12. Meditating on the Attributes of GOD
13. Puppet Scripts
14. Alcohol Ruins, JESUS Reforms, Renews & Restores!
15. Habakkuk 2:2 Christian Daily Journal, Planner & Organizer
16. ABC of GOD's Word for Handwriting Practice
17. Daily Bible Verse Handwriting Practice (Building Godly Character & Faith through Cursive Handwriting Practice!)
18. Guiding Light: Fun & Faith-Building Bible Activities for Children
19. Rejecting Grasshopper Talk: From Grasshopper to Giant-Killer-*Defeating Giants Daily!*
20. Teen Titans of Faith: *Building Courage, Determination & Christ-like-Esteem*
21. I AM Empowered: *Unleashing Divine Power with Positive Declarations*
22. Be A Solution Provider-*From Passion to Purpose*: *A Biblical Guide to Being the Answer to the World!*
23. Miracles of JESUS
24. Parables of Jesus for a Meaningful Life!
25. A Grateful Heart: Importance of Sharing Testimonies of GOD's Grace
26. Melodies of Worship to JESUS: 31 Songs of Praise & Worship From My Heart to HIS!
27. I AM SO BLESSED!
28. My Daily Cup of Energizer

29. 31 Leadership Lessons *from* Jesus- *The Supreme Leader*
30. Peace Amidst Storms: A Biblical Guide to Conquering S.T.R.E.S.S.
31. Rise Above: 20 Biblical Eagle Lessons for Life's Triumphs
32. Godly Goal Setting: *The FAITHFUL Blueprint for a Purpose-Driven Life*
33. The Profound Attributes of our Mighty GOD: Understanding the 10S's of the Almighty
34. Worship Now, Worship Forever: *A Journey from Earthly Praise to Eternal Glory*
35. Unceasing Praise & Worship: *365 Days to Worship the King*
36. The ROAR Within: *Living with Purpose and Authority through the Power of the Holy Spirit*
37. From Potential to Purpose: Unlocking and Multiplying Your Talents & Gifts for Kingdom Impact
38. Songs from the Heart: *Worshipping GOD in Your Own Tune & Melody*
39. Awakening Praise & Worship: Hebrew & Greek Words to Raise Your Praise
40. Sing a NEW Song to the LORD Everyday: *Daily Devotions of Praise & Worship to Lift Your Heart & Glorify HIS Name*
41. *The* A.R.O.M.A. of True Worship: *Creating Worship That Delights God*
42. Becoming A Kingdom Champion: *Embracing God's Call for a Life of Purpose & Victory*
43. The Busy Businessman's Daily Devotional: 366 Crisp Truths to Start Your Day Strong
44. The Teacher's Heart: *Daily Devotions for Educators*
45. Anchored! *A 31-Day Devotional for Students Facing Life's Challenges*
46. Suddenly! Unlocking Unorthodox Breakthroughs through Unusual Worship
47. Overcoming Adversity: *Lessons from the Bible for Modern Challenges*
48. LORD, Don't do it without me
49. Kingdom Leadership: *Biblical Principles for Modern Leaders*
50. Heartprints of God- *Growing God's Way:* Daily Devotions for Kids to Shine Bright
51. Send Judah First: Let your Praises Go up First to See the Mighty Move of GOD
52. DIVINE MOMENTS: *Recognizing, Embracing, Preparing, and Walking into Life-Changing Encounters with God*
53. Be a Builder in the Kingdom: *The C.E.M.E.N.T. Guide*

*to Creating a Lasting Legacy*

54. Unshakable: *Pillars of Godly Womanhood* (Pillars of Faith That Changed History)
55. Lead Like a Shepherd: *14 Essential Traits for Pastoral Excellence*
56. The Worship Leader's Arsenal: *Powerful Exhortations to Ignite Thanksgiving, Praise & Worship*
57. Women of UnShakable Faith: *31-Day Devotional for Strength, Purpose & Influence*
58. Called to Teach: *A Complete 10-Week Training Guide for Impactful VBS Teachers*
59. Strumming for the KING: Cowboy Songs of Faith & Fire
60. The Ultimate Youth Camp Playbook: *50 Bible-Centered Indoor Games to Engage, Equip, and Empower Teens*
61. Glad in HIS Presence: *David's Revelation of GOD's Love & Mercy*
62. The Spirit Behind the Sound: *52 Devotionals for Worship Teams*
63. THE COWBOY'S COMPASS: *Riding the Trail of Faith with Grit & Grace*
64. Worship as My Weapon: *Living Victoriously through the Power of Praise*

Besides regularly contributing to business & trade journals, including international ones such as the 'Creative Training Techniques' and the 'Sales News' of the U.S.A, He is also a member of several prestigious bodies & trade associations, having participated in many Conferences & Workshops in India & Overseas.

Prior to his last assignment of leading & managing a large MNC as head, Gerard had a 3-year stint in the Middle East as a Consultant with a leading British Consultancy Firm.

As the past 'Official Country Representative' for the International Business Award- 'THE STEVIES'-(the business world's own Oscar) for about 4 years- he ensured a few Indian companies that qualify for the same every year!

Gerard can be contacted at:
Email: training@Sales-Training.in,training@CollectionSkills.com
Websites:

www.Sales-Training.in
www.EtiquetteWorks.in
www.CollectionSkills.com
www.RetailSalesTraining.in
www.SalesTrainingIndia.com
www.ManualPreparation.com
www.TrainingWithPuppets.com
www.FirstContactAcademy.com
www.SalesAndMarketingRecruiter.com

## Our TRAININGS that can help your team

- ✓ **Sales Effectiveness**: Selling Skills for any Sector: Service/ Logistics/ FMCG Realty/ Insurance & Finance/ Media/ SPA's, Health Clubs & Salons/ Key Account Management, Effective Negotiation Skills/ Bid & Proposal Management Skills/ Retail Sales Training: Any Sector (Auto, Jewelry, Clothing, Luxury etc)
- ✓ **Customer Service Skills**-Complaints Handling & Customer Retention
- ✓ **Debt Prevention & Collection Skills**
- ✓ **Etiquette & Grooming**
- ✓ **Leadership & Managerial Skills**
- ✓ **Self & Personal Development Skills**: Presentation Skills/ Effective Communication Skills/Business Proposal Writing Skills/ Problem Solving & Decision Making Skills/ Empowering Secretaries-The perfect PA! (For Secretaries & PA's)/ Effective Time Management/ Teamwork & Teambuilding/ P.R.I.D.E- **P**ersonal **R**esponsibility **I**n **D**elivering **E**xcellence

www.ingramcontent.com/pod-product-compliance
Ingram Content Group UK Ltd.
Pitfield, Milton Keynes, MK11 3LW, UK
UKHW021340190726
13845UKWH00027B/643

9 788198 697448